1 HABIT™

---

100 HABITS FROM THE WORLD'S HAPPIEST ACHIEVERS

CREATED BY STEVEN SAMBLIS

Envision
media partners

1 Habit™

By Steven Samblis and many other Happy Achievers.

Published by Envision Media Press, a division of Envision Media Partners, Inc.

The publishers gratefully acknowledge the individuals that contributed to this book.

To my Daughters Lindsay and Kaitlyn

TABLE OF CONTENTS

FOREWORD

What are we all trying to achieve in life?

For years, my life was focused on being a high achiever. Success was all I could think of.

Throughout my own journey, I would go out of my way to meet respected leaders in business, culture, and social change to learn their secrets and apply it to my personal success. And that success, of course, was all measured in dollars.

But, as I set out to make this book and share these learnings, I learned something even more amazing. It turns out, my desire to achieve was on target, but I was measuring it all wrong—in dollars and cents.

No matter how much money I made, I wasn't as happy as I thought I'd be; there was always going to be someone making more. But then it dawned on me, I needed to redefine my success. Money is no longer the right measurement of success. Money, in fact, is how others measure me. Why should I give them this power?

I soon realized that happiness is how I wanted to be measured. My happiness is actually in my control. And that's when it all came together, I would rather be a "Happy Achiever™" than a "High Achiever".

I wanted to value the time with my family, my friends, my hobbies, exploring the world, and realizing my passions and dreams. To me, that is what I want to achieve.

So, with this book, I bring you the first collection of "Happy Achievers™", sharing the Habits that make each of them who they are and allow them to live the life they desire.

Enjoy this book, learn from it, and achieve your happiness.

Here's hoping that many of the readers of this book will become the contributors to future ones.

Steven Samblis

Creator of 1 Habit™

THE CREATION OF 1 HABIT™

My name is Steven Samblis, and it is my honor to present to you 1 Habit™. I hope this book will have a profound effect on your life. For you to get the most out of this book, I feel it's essential that I share with you how this book was created and more importantly, why it was created. After we will show you how to use the book to reach your maximum potential.

I say the following with absolute certainty. If you walk away and take ownership of just one of the habits in this book, It will have a profound effect on your life. I know this because when I learned the power of habits and instilled the first one into who I was, my life changed forever. I know the same can happen to you, and here is where it gets exciting. Add on another habit and another after that, and you will find your life taking off on automatic pilot to the greatness that you were born to achieve.

The Beginning...

From the time I was a young man, brand new to the business, I knew the way to be successful in my chosen field was to find successful people that came before me and do the things that they did. I was a stockbroker at the time. I would find the most successful stockbrokers in the business and study what they did every day. I then began to do the same things. I would start my day at the same time. I went to lunch at the same time. I ate dinner at the same time. I went home at the same time. I made calls when they where making calls and studied the market when they did. After the end of doing this for 6 months, I was mentally and physically fried. Obviously, something was missing.

One of my heroes at this point in my life was a stockbroker named Al Glover. Al worked with me at a Stock Brokerage firm in Cocoa Beach, Florida. It was the early 80's, and Cocoa Beach was a town where a charming house cost $150,000.00. Al was taking down a few million a year in commissions in this sleepy little beach little town.

Al's office was right across from mine so I every once in a while I would pop in his doorway and ask him how he became so successful, hoping to find the key. On one particular day, Al told me to sit down, watch, and listen. As he stood behind his desk, he picked up the phone and called a client, who he told me later was a huge client but somewhat challenging to deal with. She always over analyzed his recommendations, and by the time she was ready to pull the trigger, it was too late. "Mrs. Rooney, we have a terrific tax free bond yielding 8%, and I thought you would be interested." Al delivered the words, sat down, and shut up. It felt like an eternity went by as he sat silently on the phone, waiting for her response. "I have worked with you for many years, and during that time you have missed out on incredible opportunities which would have made you a great deal of money. This will be one of those. You have the money sitting in your Money Market, making a few points taxable. If you don't take this position, I'm not doing my job and will no longer be able to be your Financial Advisor. I will pass your account on to somebody else." Al then stopped talking and waited. Another eternity went by until Al said. "Great, we will buy $200,000.00. I will place the order for you in the morning. Great decision. Talk to you soon."

I looked at Al stunned. "You were willing to throw away one of your biggest clients if she had said no?" Al went on to tell me, every day he looked at his book of 2000 clients and picked the 5 most difficult, called them and gave them one shot to turn around the relationship or he would dump them as clients. Al had instilled in himself a habit of looking at his business every day at 6pm and making calls to remove things in it that deterred from his happiness. He said every day this one habit gave him a tremendous sense of peace. Same time every day. Most of the clients just needed that nudge to understanding what a good position they were in having him manage their money, and their attitudes and how they worked together became dramatically better. Those phone calls each day at 6pm, that single habit, had a profound effect on Al's business and happiness.

As I left Al's office, I was inspired. I was motivated and worked hard, but motivation is just the thing that gets you started. It is habits like Al's 6pm calls that keep you going and drive you down the pathway to success. Motivation is what gets you started, but it's your habits that keep you going.

Habits, once a part of you, are automatic. They don't require mental pushing and don't drain you of energy. They guide you along the right path.

I went to my office, sat on my chair, and bounced up and went right back to Al's office. "Al, this is an amazing habit, the 6pm calls. But, I don't have 2000 clients. What one habit could I make part of me that would get me to that 2000 client number?" Al took a moment and told me in a very matter of fact way. "Every night before you go home. Map out your next day. If you have clients or prospects you will want to call tomorrow, make a list before you go home. If you have a trade ticket that needs to be placed in the morning, write it out before you leave. Set yourself up for success every day by preparing the night before." Wow. He was so right! That habit sets the tone for my future success. I eventually instilled other habits now that I've learned how it all works. This, in turn, leads to me to my goal of having over 2000 clients in the next five years. From that moment on, I lived my life with the understanding "Motivation is what gets you started, but it's your habits that keep you going."

Fast forward to 2 years ago. I was filming interviews at a weekend Entrepreneurship conference for Envision TV. This incredible gathering was attended by some of the highest achievers on the planet. As we prepared to roll the interviews, a thought of my friend Al came to me. "Habits." I was about to talk to very high achievers, let's roll the dice and see if these incredibly successful people had their own habits that others could make part of their lives. I decided to ask each person the same question. One question and one question only. "If you could instantly instill in a child, 1 habit, what would it be and why?" The first answer was perfect. The second one was great. As I listened to each answer, I thought to myself, "What would my life be like if these habits were a part of who I am?" I also notice that many of these successful people from many different walks of life had the same habits.

Although I realized my videos were quite good and you can still see them at www.Envision.tv, I saw something more. As a book series, the reader can skim through a book and land on a habit and say, "That's a habit I want to make a part of me." They would spend the time, instill the habit, and once it is part of them, they can flip through the pages and find the next one.

With the idea in hand, I set out to find 100 extremely high achievers from many walks of life to contribute to our first book. I am genuinely amazed by the extraordinary people that have contributed to 1 Habit™ and have such gratitude for them believing enough in what we are doing to join us in this first book.

How to use this book…

The way to use this book is straightforward. Hard copy or digital, after you have read this Introduction, read the chapter "How to Make a Habit Your Own. Then, skim through and stop on a habit. Decide if the habit would enhance your life. If it would follow the steps to make the habit part of who you are. Once you own that habit, skim through and find your next habit. The habits from our 100 high achieving contributors are in no particular order. We did this purposefully to add some magic and serendipity to your journey. Even if you only instill just 1 habit, it can be a life changing event for you.

1 Habit™ will be a part of a growing series. We will write future 1 Habit™ books which will follow defined demographics. We will do "1 Habit™ for the Student", "1 Habit™ for the Athlete", "1 Habit™ the Single Mom" "1 Habit™ for the Entrepreneurs" and many others. We will modify the question for each topic. "If you could instantly instill in a Student, 1 habit, what would it be and why?"

I wish you the best on your path to finding the greatness that I know lives within you!

Steven Samblis – Creator of 1 Habit™ and Founder of Envision Media Partners.

HOW TO MAKE A HABIT YOUR OWN

With a small amount of work, you can build a new habit that requires little effort to maintain. After a great deal of research, we offer the top 11 things you need to do to make a habit part of who you are.

1. Let Your Habit Find You. To do this skim through the chapters and stop when you feel you are ready. Read the habit and the 'Why". If this is the one for you, it's time to begin practicing it every day until you own it.

2. Write Your Habit Down – Once you have your habit, write it down. Not just the habit but also your "Why." Knowing the reason why is as important as the habit itself. Understand why you are instilling the habit from the start. Writing the habit and the "Why" makes your ideas more clear and focuses you on the results you are looking for. Use a 3x5 card and write the habit several times and place the card around places where you will see them every day. Write a smaller version and keep it in

your purse or wallet. Once you own the habit, you can put these away.

3. Work On It Every Day– You will need to work on your habit every day. Repetition is essential if you want to make a habit stick. If you're going to start reading every day, have a book ready every day for your first month. Reading a couple of times a week will make it harder to form the habit.

4. Take a Month – A month is a perfect amount of time to commit to a change since it easily fits in your calendar.

5. Set Reminders – Set up reminders to enact your habit each day, or you might miss a few days. The best way is to set it up on your phone calendar. Have a daily reminder that pops up every day.

6. Form Triggers – This is a term from NLP (Neuro–Linguistic Programming). Triggers call forth behaviors (not thoughts or feelings). A trigger is a ritual you use right before executing your habit. If your habit was to reflect on the days as it ends, you could practice snapping your fingers each time before you begin. This action wires the habit to your brain and helps it to become an automatic action.

7. Get a Mentor – Spend more time with people who do the things you want to do. If you're going to lose weight and get in better shape, hang out with people who work out and are at their best health–wise.

8. Get a Friend to Hold You Accountable – Find a friend

who will support you and keep you motivated if you feel like giving up. (This is one of our favorites)

9. Remove Temptation – Change your World so it won't tempt you in the first month. If your habit is to eat healthy every day, Remove junk food from your house. This way, you won't find yourself struggling later as you look at your temptations right in front of you.

Side note…

Keep It Simple And Don't Try to Be Perfect – Don't try to change your world in one day. It is easy to take on too much at one time. Start small and build and do be afraid to fail. Habits will come but not all at once and not entirely. Expect bumps in the road along the way.

DEFINITION OF HABIT

Habit: A behavior pattern acquired by frequent repetition or physiologic exposure that shows itself in regularity or increased facility of performance.

CONFRONT YOUR CHALLENGES
EVERYDAY - STEVEN SAMBLIS

Habit: Confront your challenges everyday

By Steven Samblis – Creator of 1 Habit, Celebrity
Interviewer, Entrepreneur

Why: Confronting a challenge when it arrises allows you the most significant opportunity to deal with it and move on when it has the least amount of power. A challenge put aside or ignored can fester and become more daunting.

There are times when you will be in the middle of something and need to finish before taking on a new challenge. That is ok. But, if a new challenge arises and your only reason for not confronting it is fear or confusion, you need to get in there and attack it. You will be amazed at how easily you will beat new challenges just by confronting them. Once you are in the middle of dealing with them, you will also be amazed to find out that they were not really that difficult to understand or scary to deal at all.

Confronting is liberating and will build an incredible new sense of confidence in you, which will serve you well throughout the rest of your life.

 **ABOUT STEVEN SAMBLIS:** Is the founder and CEO of Envision Media Partners, Inc. Steve began his business life as a stockbroker, ranking among the top 50 rookie brokers at one of America's largest firms. He has worked with Congress defending shareholder's rights. In 1990, Steve founded "The Reason For My Success," a company that sold self–improvement programs. As the company grew, it expanded into the production of audio and video programs. Over the years, Steve has traveled North America as the keynote speaker for the Investor's Institute and launched two public companies.

His current company, Envision Media Partners, was founded with the mission "To Empower and inspire people to become their greatest selves." The company produces, acquires, and distributes personal development content across multiple platforms with an emphasis on using Virtual Reality as a learning platform for Immersive Personal Development.

2

BE RESPECTFUL TO EVERYONE YOU MEET - FRANK SHANKWITZ

The Habit: Be respectful to everyone you meet.

By Frank Shankwitz – Founder of the Make–A–Wish Foundation

Why: You have heard the expression "Treat others as you would like to be treated"? Being respectful pays big dividends. It's a micro action in the "pay it forward" movement. When you are respectful to others, you will see them light up, and most will be respectful in turn. Being treated with respect can be life changing to some. This simple habit can put smiles on the faces of people around you and will make your world a warmer place.

About Frank: Frank Shankwitz is best known as the Creator, Co-Founder, and first President/CEO of the

 Make-A-Wish Foundation, an extraordinary charity that grants the wishes to children with life-threatening illnesses. From humble beginnings, the Make-A-Wish Foundation is now a global organization that grants a child's wish somewhere in the world on an average of every 28 minutes. Frank is a U.S. Air Force veteran and has a long and distinguished career in law enforcement. He began as a Arizona Highway Patrol Motorcycle Officer, and retired as a Homicide Detective with the Arizona Department of Public Safety, with 42 years of service. Frank has been featured in numerous publications and television programs, and has received several awards, including the White House Call To Service Award from both President George W. Bush and President Donald J. Trump, and the "Making A Difference In the World" award from the U.S. Military Academy at West Point. In 2015 Frank joined six U.S. Presidents as well as Nobel Prize winners and industry leaders as a recipient of the Ellis Island Medal of Honor. In December 2015, following his commencement address, Frank was presented with an Honorary Doctorate Degree, Doctor of Public Service, from The Ohio State University. In December 2015, Frank was identified as one of the "10 Most Amazing Arizonans", in a front-page article in the Arizona Republic newspaper. In January 2016, Frank was identified in a Forbes Magazine article as a "Forbes Top Ten Keynote Speaker". In April 2017, Frank was presented the Unite4:Humanity Celebrity ICON Social Impact Award, joining past recipients Matthew

McConaughey and Morgan Freeman. In February 2018, Frank shared the stage with Matthew McConaughey at Universal Studios at the LA City Gala and was presented the first City Gala Hero Award. Frank's new book, "Wish Man", was re-released in September, 2018 and is available at Amazon.com. In May 2019, following his commencement address, Frank was presented with an Honorary Doctorate Degree, Doctor of Law, from St. Norbert College. In June 2019, Frank joined 89 celebrities, when he received his "STAR" on the Las Vegas Walk of Fame. Frank's life story, "Wish Man", a feature motion picture, was released in June 2019. Frank is a board member on several non-profits, including U.S. Vets, The Wounded Blue, and Broadway Hearts.

3

FOLLOW CPC: CLUES, PATTERNS, AND CHOICES - DR. GREG REID

The Habit: Follow CPC: Clues, Patterns, and Choices

By Dr. Greg Reid – Entrepreneur, Keynote Speaker, and Bestselling Author

Why: I have a friend, Mark Anthony Bates, who has a philosophy called CPC: clues, patterns, and choices. We believe it is the secret of all awareness and accountability for success and failure.

Let's say you have a business meeting and the client shows up late. Well, that's a clue that something may be off. The reason he provides for being late may or may not be true —who knows? It's just a clue.

The first meeting went well enough to warrant a second

one. On the second meeting the client ends up being late again. Suddenly the clue has turned into a pattern.

Now it's up to you to make a choice based on this pattern: Are you going to continue to do business with him, get upset, or even confront him about it and demand he show greater respect for your time if you are going to work together?

The reality is that you can't and shouldn't attempt to change the person who was late. It's not your responsibility. He is who he is. Instead, it's your responsibility—your choice—whether you are going to accept the lateness or do business with someone else.

The same goes for friendships. If you pay attention to the clues and patterns, you get to choose to stay or leave. If you decide to keep going, you can only blame yourself if those negative patterns disrupt your life.

Positive patterns lead to a life of ease and grace.

About Greg: Dr. Greg Reid, who received his honorary Ph.D. in literature, is considered one of the top five keynote speakers by Forbes and Entrepreneur. He has been published in more than 70 books, which have been translated into 45 languages. Among his bestselling books are Wealth Made Easy, Stickability, and Three Feet from Gold. He can be found having a great time brewing up inspiration, occasionally breaking into song and dance, and being of contribution to those around him.

4

LEARN FROM FAILURE - JOHN SHIN

The Habit: Learn from failure

By John Shin – Author, Speaker, Philanthropist

Why: This is a habit that I have used my entire life. It's simple and just takes an extra beat to accomplish, but can create fantastic growth and improvement in anyone's life.

This is 1 Habit that also builds a strong sense of humility in people. Because it makes them take a hard look at themselves and fearlessly look at their flaws.

The way it works is straightforward. If I ever fail, I ask myself, "What could I have done to make this better?". Then when a similar situation comes up, I correct my previous mistake.

Another benefit to this habit is it requires you to think before you act or speak rather than react. Think about this. How many times in your life would things have turned out better if you had taken an extra beat before reacting or speaking?

The practice of this habit is simple. As an example, when I was in school, if I don't get a good grade on a test, I ask myself if I was prepared. If I weren't, then next time, I would prepare better to get a better grade.

Learning from failure will make every stumble a learning event. So many people coast through life, not paying attention to each opportunity to grow and become better. This habit will open your eyes to the life you are living and all the potential before you.

 **ABOUT JOHN:** John Shin is a Korean American entrepreneur, philanthropist, and the Executive Producer of "Think and Grow Rich the Legacy" movie. He founded The Think and Grow Rich Legacy World Tour Inc. John is also the author of "How Rich Asians Think," which is s Think and Grow Rich publication. Which is an official publication of the Napoleon Hill Foundation.

John Shin was 3 months old when he and his family immigrated to Los Angeles in the late 1960s. As early as 8 years old, he knew that he wanted to start a business. In grade school, John made his first $100 on candy sales with a goal to earn $150 to purchase his first bike. He got his bike, and this began his entrepreneurial spirit.

Growing up in California as a young 6–year boy, John would get bullied and to protect himself, he began to study Tae Kwon–Do, Judo, and Hapkido. He continued to train and compete, which he would go on to win at the State and Regional level competitions by age 11. At 14 years old, John competed Nationally and won Gold. He then went on to compete at the World Games, Pan American Games and tried out for the 1988 Olympic Team.

For 25 years, he has empowered people to achieve peak performance in business, sales, money, teams, relationships, and life. He has mentored and trained thousands of people around the country to become successful business owners. His greatest joy is to teach and train businesses to grow and achieve real success.

He believes that mentorship, training, and coaching are core key values for a successful life.

John founded a progressive sales, and personal growth training company made up of professional mentors and business builders who work one–on–one with individuals, businesses, and major corporations to help them achieve growth in any economy.

He is also the Co–Founder of a non–profit organization called "ALL FOR ONE," which provides child prosperity centers for children around the world. Together with the organization, they have built and created 10 orphanages in 6 countries like Uganda, Philippines, Nicaragua, Vietnam, China, and India and have helped over 1,000 kids live within their orphanages.

His clients range from the individual person seeking simple financial advice to Doctors, Lawyers, Fortune 500 companies, federal credit unions, Hollywood celebrities, and professional athletes (NBA, MLB, and NFL).

Today, he commands a sales force of nearly 9,600 agents, practices in 42 states, with 120 offices throughout the United States.

TREAT PEOPLE THE WAY THEY WANT & NEED TO BE TREATED - DR. TONY ALESSANDRA

The Habit: Treat people the way they want & need to be treated

By Dr. Tony Alessandra – NSA Speakers Hall of Fame Member and Bestselling Author

Why: I believe in refining The Golden Rule, Do Unto Others as You Would Have Them Do Unto You, to take into consideration the feelings of the other person. Notice I didn't say break the rule. I redefine it into The Platinum Rule –– "Do Unto Others As They Would Have You Do Unto Them." Treat others the way they want to be treated. By "platinum," I don't mean to imply "better." I simply want to capture the true spirit or actual intention of the Golden Rule, so we consider and respond appropriately to the other person's needs. We can learn to treat different people differently, according to their needs, not ours. That leads to greater understanding and acceptance. Let me explain. When you treat others as you want to be treated, you can end up offending others who have different needs, wants, and expectations from you. So when you apply the Golden Rule verbatim, there's a much greater chance of triggering conflict over chemistry. Yes, you heard it right. Following the Golden Rule verbatim means treating others from your point of view. That means you naturally tend to speak in the way you are most comfortable listening or sell to others the way you like to be sold or manage the way you want others to direct you.

 **ABOUT DR. TONY:** Dr. Tony Alessandra has a street–wise, college–smart perspective on business, having been raised in the housing projects of NYC to eventually realizing success as a graduate professor of marketing, Internet entrepreneur, business author, and hall–of–fame keynote speaker. He earned a BBA from Notre Dame, an MBA from the Univ. of Connecticut and his Ph.D. in marketing in 1976 from Georgia State University.

Tony is CEO of Assessments 24x7 LLC, a company that offers a variety of online assessments, including the widely used DISC profile, the Hartman HPV, Motivators (Values/PIAV) assessment, and several 360° effectiveness assessments.

He is also a prolific author with 31 books translated into over 50 foreign language editions, including the newly revised, best–selling The NEW Art of Managing People; Charisma; The Platinum Rule; Collaborative Selling; and Communicating at Work.

He is featured in over 100 audio/video programs and films, including DISC Relationship Strategies; The Dynamics of Effective Listening; and Gaining the EDGE in Competitive Selling. He is also the originator of the internationally recognized behavioral style assessment tool – The Platinum Rule®.

Dr. Alessandra was inducted into the NSA Speakers Hall of Fame in 1985. In 2009, he was inducted as one of the "Legends of the Speaking Profession;" in 2010–2014, he was selected 5 times as one of the Speakers.com Top 5 Sales/ Marketing/ Customer Service Speakers by Speaking.com; in 2010, Tony was elected into the inaugural class of the Top Sales World Sales Hall of Fame; in 2012, he was voted one of the Top 50 Sales & Marketing Influencers; and also in 2012, Dr. Tony was voted the #1 World's Top Communication Guru.

Recognized by Meetings & Conventions Magazine as "one of America's most electrifying speakers," Tony's polished style, powerful message, and proven ability as a consummate business strategist consistently earn rave reviews and loyal clients.

6

STAND UP FOR THOSE WHO CANNOT STAND UP FOR THEMSELVES - RANDY SUTTON

Habit: Stand up for those who cannot stand up for themselves

By Lt. Randy Sutton (Ret) – Founder/CEO of The Wounded Blue

Why: When I was just a child, my parents instilled in me an ethical "habit" that has, in reality, touched the lives of thousands of people in my role as a Law Enforcement Officer and also a journalist. That "habit" was to stand up for those who could not stand up for themselves. The bullied, the shy and withdrawn, the loner or the outcast who simply because they were viewed as "different" were treated cruelly. Cruelty can, unfortunately, become contagious, but it only takes one person to break the power of others who inflict emotional hurt on another. Standing up for someone by word or deed can alter lives. Admittedly, I endured a little redirected pain and discomfort along the way, but in reflection, could there be any greater honor than to make a difference in someone's life through courage and compassion? I'll let you answer THAT question.

 **ABOUT RANDY:** Randy Sutton is the National Spokesman for BLUE LIVES MATTER, the largest grass-roots law enforcement support organization in America. He is a 34–year police veteran. Randy is also the founder of The Wounded Blue Foundation. The foundation was created to assist Law Enforcement Officers who are injured physically and or psychologically in the line of duty to help them obtain the treatment and medical/financial benefits they are entitled to. The organization also is there to advocate for stronger protections under state and federal law and provide emergency funds to injured officers when circumstances dictate the need.

7

LIVE EACH DAY LEARNING TO UNDERSTAND YOURSELF - MARIE ROBERTS DE LA PARRA

The Habit: Live each day learning to understand yourself

By Marie Roberts De La Parra – Chief Emotional Officer

Why: For many, during the educational journey, the main point that is instilled in you and commands your focus is to "get the good grade, the A." What I have found that is the key to learning, is to understand. To build your wealth of knowledge and by doing so, getting the "A" is the outcome. Promoting understanding increases the level to learn and establishes internal power. Setting the individualized foundation for developing the intuitiveness to best use your unique talents, gifts, and skill. The ability to do you well!

About Marie: Marie Roberts De La Parra is the founder of Wait a Green Minute and the creator of the Life Energy Management System. She has received appointments to the California Department of Consumer Affairs, Bureau of Private Post–Secondary Education Advisory Committee, and to the U.S. E.P.A. Environmental Finance Advisory Board in Washington D.C. As an (8) year loan committee member for 1(8) California state certified financial development corporations, Nor–Cal F.D.C, Marie has assisted over 2000 small businesses with gaining access to over 200 million dollars in financial capital. Additionally, she maintains an advisory board member seat at the University of San Francisco B.A.S.E. program (Black Achievement Success & Engagement), where she is obtaining a doctorate in Organization and Leadership with a minor in Learning and Instruction. She has worked with the U.S. Department of Commerce participating in events in Spain, the Canary Islands; and with West African countries. Ms. Roberts De La Parra is a Fellow of the Global Citizen Alliance in Salzburg, Austria, and is committed to global educational, community, and economic development.

8

NEVER LIE TO YOURSELF (BE SELF-AWARE!) - DR. REBECCA HEISS

The Habit: Never lie to yourself (Be self–aware!)

By Dr. Rebecca Heiss – CEO/Founder Icueity
Professional Speaker, Author, Director Envision Media
Partners

Why: We are all guilty of some level of cognitive dissonance – Imagine the story you tell yourself about being in control of your eating habits as you grab that 2nd donut. When our beliefs don't match our behaviors, we allow our subconscious brains to justify our actions. We make up a story (I'll work it off at the gym later) or change our original value statements (I never wanted to lose those 5 lbs anyway!). Only when you sit with the discomfort and vulnerability that self–awareness brings will you be able to create your path toward greatness consciously.

 **About Rebecca:** After earning her Ph.D. with research designated as "transformative" by the National Science Foundation, Dr. Rebecca Heiss went on to hold multiple appointments in academia, applying her research to solve practical problems in overcoming what she refers to as "biological ghosts" – subconscious behaviors that haunt modern life. She founded a stress hormone consultation company, Biologic Balance, and is currently launching a new self–awareness, 360–review app, called Icueity, to help every individual reach her/his full potential.

She has been honored to speak internationally on her work, including multiple TEDx talks, and has found her calling in helping others recognize the power of biological applications in their lives. Rebecca lives in South Carolina with her spoiled rotten dog named Bird, and tries every day to live her life motto: "spread happy."

9

PRACTICE PHYSICAL FITNESS EVERY DAY - MARK TUFO

The Habit: Practice physical fitness every day

By Mark Tufo – International Bestselling Author

Why: This leads to self–confidence and the belief that you can do anything, succeed at any task. The resulting confidence is a trait that will bleed into every facet of your life.

A strong body goes hand in hand with a strong mind. Team sports lead to self–esteem, the desire to cooperate and achieve socially, and find leadership abilities. Of all the qualities that lead to success, none is more important to walk through this world with that self–confidence; fitness is a great way to develop it.

ABOUT MARK: Mark Tufo is an International Bestselling Author of Horror, Science Fiction, Apocalyptic Survivalist Fiction, Young Adult Dystopian, and Paranormal fiction. He has penned over forty books, sold over a million copies, and been translated into three languages. His books have won numerous awards and have spent weeks in the number one slot for Horror on the Amazon charts.

His longest running series, Zombie Fallout, now in its twelfth installment, is currently being adapted for television, at the anticipation of millions of fans.

10

STAY IN THE PRESENT - JOHN DAVIS

The Habit: Stay in the present

By John Davis – The Corporate Action Hero

Why: We all set goals for the future. Sometimes those goals can seem dauntingly large. Vast successes are the result of making small present moments successful and having each build upon the last. When you stay firmly in your present moment, your goals won't seem overwhelming or unattainable. Create small successes that are in alignment with the larger goal, and that larger goal will materialize in your present. Also, If a small moment is less than successful, don't waste the next moment beating yourself up.

ABOUT JOHN: John is a dynamic speaker, accomplished leader, and expert in inspiring people to peak performances. He has over 20 years of experience speaking for Fortune 500 clients and a broad swath of industries including healthcare, financial, insurance, retail, and the military at hundreds of conferences, seminars, and retreats.

John's background in peak performance stems from his work as a fight director and stunt coordinator for stage and film as well as his work for the military. His ability to engage individuals, unite teams, and drive change was instrumental in increasing the profitability of three regional theme parks by more than 60% in under six months of his direction.

During this time, John was also a professional comedian who brought his unique entertainments to bear for our military on six USO tours to the front lines of both Iraq and Afghanistan. Inspired by his work with the military, John felt he had to find deeper meaning in his work, and began focusing on helping others reach their chosen potentials. This new direction led him to become a college professor at Oberlin College in Ohio.

While teaching at Oberlin, John's fascination with personal development led him to Study the neuroscience of performance. He developed peak performance protocols based upon the fight or flight response called the "Five F Protocols."

11

END EACH DAY WITH GRATITUDE - EILEEN MCDARGH

The Habit: End each day with gratitude

By Eileen McDargh – Award–winning Author and Speaker

Why: Imagine what positive thoughts enter one's mind if, at the end of the day, she is asked: "what happened today to make you thankful or happy?"

Living in a world that often focuses on the negative, going to sleep with such a thought begins to develop a needed mindset: optimism.

ABOUT EILEEN: Since 1980, Eileen McDargh has helped organizations and individuals transform the life of their

 business and the business of their lives through conversations that matter and connections that count. She has become known as a master facilitator, an award–winning author, and an internationally recognized keynoter and executive coach.

She draws upon practical business know–how, life's experiences and years of consulting to major national and international organizations that have ranged from global pharmaceuticals to the US Armed Forces, from health care associations to religious institutions. Her programs are content–rich, interactive, provocative and playful— even downright hilarious.

In 2019, Global Gurus International, a British–based provider of resources for leadership, communication and sales training, also ranked her FIRST as one of the World's Top 30 Communication Professionals following a global survey of 22,000 business professionals.

12

EMBRACING DELAYED GRATIFICATION - DR. TODD DEWETT

The Habit: Embracing delayed gratification.

By Dr. Todd Dewett – Author, Educator, Speaker

Why: This is the ability to delay the consumption of something you enjoy until you have achieved a particular self–defined goal. For example, I will not eat out at a restaurant until I have reached my monthly savings goal. Or, I will not buy a new car until I receive the promotion. Or maybe, I will not take a vacation until I successfully wrap up the project. The ability to consciously choose to not indulge in something you want (and could have right now) so that you can savor it later when it is "earned" is priceless. Over time, this helps you build a disciplined focus and ability to persevere in the face of challenges effectively.

Most importantly, your eventual indulgences are so much more enjoyable!

 **About Todd:** Dr. Todd Dewett is a Bestselling Author at LinkedIn Learning, a TEDx speaker, and an Inc. Magazine Top 100 leadership speaker. A former award–winning professor (Ph.D. Organizational Behavior, Texas A&M University) and alumnus of Andersen Consulting and Ernst & Young, Todd has delivered over 1,000 speeches and created a body of educational work enjoyed by millions of professionals around the globe.

13

EXHIBIT THE HIGHEST LEVELS OF BEARING - ERIK THERWANGER

The Habit: Exhibit the highest levels of bearing.

By Erik Therwanger – U.S. Marine, Sales Professional and Entrepreneur

Why: As a U.S. Marine, I learned the deeper meaning of the leadership trait, bearing. In the civilian business sector, I find it one of the most underutilized words. But this could be the greatest way to earn the respect of your peers. Bearing is all about how you carry and conduct yourself. It is a reflection of how you represent yourself, your team, and your organization. Bearing is contagious, and when you exhibit it at the highest levels, you will encourage others to do the same.

ABOUT ERIK: Erik Therwanger is the Founder of Think GREAT, a specialized business consulting firm that specializes in leadership development, strategic planning, and sales combustion. He uniquely combines his experiences as a U.S. Marine, executive business leader, sales professional, and entrepreneur to help organizations achieve new levels of success. He is also the Author of the Think GREAT Collection, a series of books dedicated to personal and professional growth. Erik is also the Founder of the Think GREAT Foundation, which awards scholarships to military spouses.

14

CONSTANTLY BE OF SERVICE TO OTHERS - BILLY ARCEMENT

The Habit: Constantly be of service to others.

By Billy Arcement – The Candid Cajun, Leadership Speaker and Consultant

Why: St. Francis of Assisi said, "For it is in giving that we receive." What a wonderful gift to give with no thought of the return to us. Teaching, helping, sharing our talents, skills, and knowledge can be life–changing to us as well as others. It's not a secondary role but one of pure humility. It actually takes a powerful, self–confident individual to give of themselves to others with no fear of loss. Honest, trustworthy, transparent, and respectful character comes with serving others. Give to receive. That's how life works.

About Billy: Billy Arcement is known as "The Candid Cajun" for his real world, challenging, but caring conversations. He shares relevant and cutting–edge information. His expertise focuses on organizational and personal leadership strategies. His messages are memorable, energizing, and filled with real–world examples. His unique and special blend of "Cajun Humor" makes his keynotes and seminar training sessions entertaining and enlightening. It is learning and laughter, a proven, winning combination. Audiences across America appreciate his sincerity, candid commentary, and passion. It's all about them, not him! A 38–year member of the National Speakers Association he is also a charter member and past president of the New Orleans Chapter. In 2004, the Chapter created "The Billy Arcement Leadership Award" because of his many contributions leading to the growth of the Chapter. Billy was elected to and served 12 years on his local school board. His state–wide peers also elected him state president of the Louisiana School Boards Association. A prolific writer, he is the author of four books and over 300 articles on personal and organizational leadership strategies.

15

SPEND LESS THAN YOU MAKE - MARK SANBORN

The Habit: Spend less than you make.

By Mark Sanborn – International Bestselling Author

Why: My dad taught me this habit as a child, and it has served me better than any other financial practice. I've tried to teach it to my sons, and it would be the one habit I would instantly instill in any child to help create success for him or her in the future. This prevents burdensome debt and provides the foundation for savings and security. Today culture often encourages people to live beyond their means, attain credit cards they don't need to pay down and to live for the moment. The advice my father taught me can make anyone successful and wealthy if applied well.

ABOUT MARK: Mark Sanborn is the president of Sanborn & Associates, Inc., an idea lab for leadership development and turning ordinary into extraordinary. He is listed as one of the top leadership experts in the world. Mark has given over 2600 presentations in every state and fourteen countries. He has authored 8 books and more than two dozen videos and audio training programs. His programs are taught by Crestcom International in 90 countries, and he is an adjunct professor at the University of Memphis. Mark is a member of the Speaker Hall of Fame and is a past president of the National Speakers Association.

16

TALK TO STRANGERS - KATHY GRUVER

The Habit: Talk to strangers

By Dr. Kathy Gruver – Author, Speaker and Educator

Why: I know it's against what you were taught as a child, but by being open and friendly to people around you, you open yourself up to opportunities, information, and possibilities.

By engaging in small talk with people around you, you can open the door to new relationships, business opportunities, and needed information. We create our own 'good luck' and people who are open, extroverted and conversational tend to get more breaks and find more success.

ABOUT KATHY: Kathy Gruver, Ph.D. has graced stages on four continents (including TEDx), three cruise ships and a handful of islands. Her combination of humor, performance background, real–life experience, and formal education makes her a well–rounded, in–demand speaker. She hosts the TV show based on her first book, The Alternative Medicine Cabinet and has earned her Ph.D. in Natural Health. Dr. Gruver is the twelve–time award–winning author of seven books including, Conquer Your Stress, Workplace Wellness, Conquer your Stress at Work, and Journey of Healing.

She has studied mind/body medicine at the famed Benson–Henry Institute for Mind–Body Medicine at Harvard, and has been featured as an expert in numerous publications including Glamour, Fitness, Time, WebMD, Prevention, Huffington Post and Dr. Oz's The Good Life, and has appeared on over 250 radio & TV shows including Lifetime, NPR, CBS Radio and SkyNews London. In 2015 she had the privilege of creating a stress reduction program for the US Military and has been studying psychology and human behavior her entire life. She is also the co–host of the new Fire and Earth Podcast. For fun and stress relief Gruver does hip hop and flying trapeze.

17

WEAVE MINDFULNESS INTO YOUR LIFE - JOY RAINS

The Habit: Weave mindfulness into your life

By Joy Rains – Mindfulness Speaker and Author

Why: Want to reduce stress? Practice mindfulness. Instead of focusing on the past or future, pay attention to the "here and now," even for just a moment. When you walk, feel the soles of your feet as they touch the ground. When you shower, listen to the sounds of running water. When you take a breath, notice the coolness of the air as you inhale and its warmth as you exhale. Mindful living is excellent for your health—and it's simple to practice!

 **ABOUT JOY:** Joy Rains is a leading mindfulness speaker and author of two books: Meditation Illuminated: Simple Ways to Manage Your Busy Mind, a primer for beginning meditators and Ignite Your Sales Power! Mindfulness Skills for Sales Professionals, a book to help sales professionals develop a positive, customer–focused approach.

Joy has been a featured presenter at The U.S. Food and Drug Administration, Marriott Corporation, Sinai Hospital, and Allstate Insurance. She's a widely referenced media source on mindfulness, quoted in publications including U.S. News and World Report, Reader's Digest, Healthline, and Work Design Magazine.

18

BE AN EXPRESSION OF HUMILITY IN BOTH WORD AND DEED - LINDA ZANDER

The Habit: Be an expression of humility in both word and deed.

By: Linda Zander – Member of the Forbes Coaches Council

Why: Humility is the virtue that allows you to connect to others, keep an open mind, and achieve a pleasing personality. When you act and speak humbly, others feel heard, safe, and valued, which creates a supportive environment where caring and sharing co–creates a more compassionate and sustainably successful World for one and all.

About Linda: Linda Zander is the Founder and CEO of Success Pros Online and the We Give Program. The We Give Program offers free success coaching to those in

need worldwide. Its mission statement is that no person, regardless of gender, geography, disability, race, religion, or economic status be denied the opportunity to Succeed – and that support shall be easily accessible to all. At Success Pros Online, Linda and her global team of pros are helping people to receive the help they need when they need it, affordably and by eliminating oppressive contracts, membership fees, and wait times. Through relentlessly living her own holistic model of success known as the Maximum Riches Formula™, Linda achieved success in all areas of her life. She became a self–made multimillionaire before the age of 40, overturned a fatal health diagnosis, became a medaled amateur athlete and gained an international presence as an adept advisor on the topic of sustainable wealth and well–being. Linda is a member of the Forbes Coaches Council, a Forbes Contributor, and Certified Science of Success Instructor. In 2006, Linda received the City of Los Angele's Certificate of Recognition for Courage and Determination and dubbed "An inspiration to all and an Angel in Our City of Angels."

19

LOOK FOR WAYS TO SAY YES - SUSAN SHARP

The Habit: Look for ways to say "Yes"

By Susan Sharp – Artist, Speaker and Author

Why: There's a good reason to say no to lots of different things. Sometimes we say no, however, because we don't have the self–confidence to say yes or we dismiss ideas with lots of complexity because we just can't see how that could be done. But what if you looked for ways to say yes? What if you looked for ways to make complex ideas a reality? Most everyone else is going to choose the fastest and easiest way—by saying no. Be a yes person––not to everything and everyone—but believe in yourself enough to see the impossible as possible. Have confidence in your crazy, improbable ideas, your dreams, and your vision. Whoever thought we'd have giant outdoor sculptures in public parks, cellphones or online education? Someone did——Someone that dared to ponder an idea rather than dismissing it! Think bigger. Ask big questions. Embrace yes—it's harder, but it's much more rewarding.

 **ABOUT SUSAN:** Susan Sharp is an abstract artist, theatre professor, speaker, playwright and author who's crazy about big ideas and dreams. For over 20 years, she has encouraged students and audiences to find and nurture their creativity. As an artist whose work has appeared in numerous galleries and on the set of Orange is the New Black, she speaks with people all the time who want to be more creative or live more creatively. She founded asharpdifference.com as a platform to inspire creative work and big ideas for those in a rut. Through her workshops and keynote speaking, Susan wants to shake up the conventional notion of what it is to be happy, creative, and productive. Susan's books, The Change 13th ed., Mid–Life Wisdom and Frotter Spires all share the message of believing in self to live a happier life. Growing up in rural Iowa, Susan has been irrevocably changed by the endless possibilities of wide open spaces.

20

DRINK AND EAT ENOUGH WATER - JOHN AYO

The Habit: Drink and eat enough water

By John Ayo – Wellness Speaker and Author

Why: We can achieve amazing things in our life (per the other habits in this book) when we have our health. However, when we don't have our health, nothing else matters. Our bodies are mostly water, and the simple habit of drinking more water (as well as eating it in the form of fruits and vegetables) is one of the BEST things you can do for your health.

About John: John is a Professional Speaker, Naturopath, and Author focused on inspiring and empowering professionals to stay energized, healthy, and balanced while traveling. John spent 30+ years working in sales and

sales training at IBM, where he achieved remarkable results as a seller and speaker. He has taught more than 4,000 people in 26 countries about his secrets to better health on the road (and back at home)! As a result of his extensive travel experience, he wrote a book called Travel Balance, that helps business travelers stay energized, healthy, and balanced while traveling. John is a traditional naturopath and has a thriving natural health practice in Plano, Tx. John holds a BS in Civil Engineering, an MBA and a Doctorate in Naturopathy (ND). He spends countless hours researching diverse health issues, with a strong desire to find solutions that can impact the lives of people, especially as it relates to business travel.

21

START A DAILY SPIRITUAL PRACTICE - RICK BRONIEC

The Habit: Start a daily spiritual practice.

By Rick Broniec – Facilitator, Coach, Speaker and Amazon Bestselling Author

W hy: Starting out your day with a few moments of reflection, prayer, meditation or breath–work can ground you, remind you of what you're grateful for and connect you with the sense that you are part of a greater whole that supports your life. This essential practice centers you in peace and power to start your day with clarity, energy, and a smile on your face.

About Rick: Rick Broniec, M.Ed. is a writer, inspirational speaker, coach, and workshop facilitator. He has been a pre–eminent leader of men's training since 1988, having

facilitated men's personal growth and leadership workshops on five continents and ten countries for thousands of men.

Rick is an Amazon bestseller author of The Seven Generations Story: An Incentive to Heal Yourself, Your Family and the Planet and A Passionate Life: 7 Steps for Reclaiming Your Passion, Purpose and Joy and has co–written (With Leonard Szymczak) Wake Up, Grow Up and Show Up: Calling Men Into the 21st Century.

ALWAYS BE TOLERANT OF OTHER PEOPLE'S OPINIONS - GAURAV BHALLA

The Habit: Always be tolerant of other people's opinions

By Gaurav Bhalla – Ph.D. Transforming Businesses and Lives: Speaker, Author, Coach

 hy: Let Rudyard Kipling answer this for us.

"If you can keep your head when all about you.

Are losing theirs and blaming it on you,

If you can trust yourself when all men doubt you,

But make allowance for their doubting too;"

EVERYONE IS ENTITLED to their opinion and point–of–view. But what they are not entitled to is thinking theirs is the only opinion and point–of–view that matters. No individual has a monopoly of the truth. Each one of us has only a slice of it. Regardless of the nature and strength of our point–of–view, there's always another way of looking at and interpreting the reality that surrounds us. Always.

Yes, we must trust ourselves, we must have the confidence and courage to back our convictions. But we must also have the tolerance to hear and understand why others may or may not see eye–to–eye with us. This one simple act – *making allowance for their doubting too* – can make the world a more accepting and a friendlier place. Definitely worth shaking hands on, definitely a habit worth cultivating.

ABOUT GAURAV: Dr. Gaurav Bhalla is a globally acclaimed leadership and marketing strategy specialist. The developer of the school of Soulful LeadershipTM, his purpose and passion is to inspire organizations, teams, and individuals to achieve greater professional success and personal fulfillment by leading with their humanity, not just their executive brilliance.

He facilitates this transformation through entertaining and insightful keynote speeches and talks, through thought–provoking workshops, and human–centric coaching. These offerings have guided thousands of people around the world Re–imagine, Re–purpose, and Relaunch their leadership, business, and life's journeys. His skills, reputation, and experience were recognized and rewarded in 2016, when he won the "Executive Education Specialist of the Year" award, presented by AI Global Media, a UK–based media and information company.

During his 40+ years global career, he has worked with clients, such as Glaxo Smith Kline, Caterpillar, Deloitte, Hallmark, IBM, Maersk, and Marriott, and with leading B–Schools, such as Georgetown, Duke, Singapore Management University, GIBS–South Africa, and Indian School of Business.

Published in both business and literature, his leading–edge thinking is reflected in his HBR article, "Rethinking Marketing," and his newest book, "Awakening A Leader's Soul: Learnings Through Immortal Poems," a 21st century visionary manifesto on Soulful LeadershipTM.

What sets Gaurav apart from other speakers, coaches, and authors are his thinker–doer mindset, his passion for translating knowledge into action, and his purpose that values the humanity of people over their executive brilliance.

23

ALWAYS KEEP YOUR WORD - BONNIE LOW-KRAMEN

The Habit: Always keep your word

By Bonnie Low–Kramen – Author

Why: Words matter – a lot. We trust people we believe and can count on, and this is how the strongest relationships are built. Don't say things you don't mean and don't tell you will do something and not do it. Become known as the person whose words you can take to the bank and who follows up. If you speak it or write it, the act is as good as done. This will separate you from many other people.

About Bonnie: Bonnie is a celebrity personal assistant turned entrepreneur and business owner who now employs an executive assistant. For 25 years, Bonnie worked with Oscar–winning actress Olympia Dukakis. In

2011, she left this dream job to take on a new one of traveling the world teaching and speaking, and now she has worked in 14 countries. One of the most respected leaders in the administrative profession, Bonnie is at the center of the movement to end workplace bullying and to close the wage gap between women and men. Bonnie is the bestselling author of "Be the Ultimate Assistant." And she is Adam's mom.

24

MAKE EVERYTHING YOU SAY A PRESENTATION - BRIDGETT MCGOWEN

The Habit: Make everything you say a presentation.

By Bridgett McGowen – Awarded
International Professional Speaker

Why: Think of the last time you made a presentation or gave a speech. You were very careful of the words you selected. You practiced over and over and over again. You wanted to ensure you struck the right tone, gave the right impression, and made the audience experience that "wow" feeling! Why reserve that only for presentations made to the masses?! Endeavor to provide everyone you encounter that "wow" feeling. Stand tall, make eye contact, keep your shoulders back, and speak to everyone – EVERYONE – as if he/she is the most important person in the room. And when you do that ... when you make everything you say a presentation, so many things happen ... your confidence gets an incredible boost, you make your listeners feel special, and you demonstrate to others you care and that you are in control and in command of your message. But most importantly, when you make everything you say a presentation with the intent of shining the spotlight on others to make them feel extraordinary, guess who else ends up shining. YOU!

ABOUT BRIDGETT: Bridgett McGowen is an award-winning international professional speaker; the founder of BMcTALKS, an Arizona-based presentation skills firm; and the author of *REAL TALK: What Other Experts Won't Tell You About How to Make Presentations That Sizzle.* She is a native Texan and has appeared on programs alongside notable figures such as former President Barack Obama, Deepak Chopra, and Oprah Winfrey. Bridgett has made hundreds of presentations to thousands of professionals all around the globe, consistently moving her audiences to bubble over with laughter and enthusiasm.

25

BE SITUATIONALLY AWARE AT ALL TIIMES - ROBERT SICILIANO

The Habit: Be situationally aware at all times

By Robert Siciliano – CSP, Bestselling Author

Why: By making awareness a habit, you see 10 times more of the good life has to offer, and for your security, you'll see more of the bad. This means no matter where you are, no matter what you are doing, be fully aware of the situation you are in, the people in it and the activity going on around the perimeter of your body. People who are situationally aware, live in the moment and embrace life more comprehensively. They see an opportunity, and they perceive danger. They are on top of what is new, and ahead of what is next.

ABOUT ROBERT: Robert Siciliano is a CSP, the #1 Bestselling Amazon.com Author and CEO of Safr.Me, may get your attention with his fun engaging tone and approachable personality— but he is serious about teaching you and your audience fraud prevention and personal security. Robert is also security expert and private investigator fiercely committed to informing, educating and empowering people so they can protect themselves and their loved ones from violence and crime in their everyday lives, both in their physical and virtual interactions.

26

BE ABLE TO LAUGH AT YOURSELF - JOE SCHMIT

The Habit: Be able to laugh at yourself

By Joe Schmit – Speaker, Author, Award Winning Broadcaster

Why: Life is tough enough, so don't take yourself so seriously. We all slip, we all trip, we all forget, we all say stupid things, and we all have the human condition, so we screw up once in a while. When you do, can laugh at yourself. Self–deprecation is a trait that makes you more authentic and likable. It's a habit that will help turn stress into joy.

About Joe: Joe Schmit is an author, award–winning broadcaster, community leader, and popular keynote speaker. His 1ST book "Silent Impact" Influence Through Purpose, Persistence, and Passion is now in its 2nd

edition. His new book "The Impact Blueprint," A Step by Step Journey to a Life of Significance, is a deep dive into how to lead your professional and personal life with impact. He joined KSTP–TV in 1985 and has won 18 Emmys from the National Television Academy. He was also honored with a National Headliner Award in 2001. Joe is also a regular on 1500ESPN radio. Before joining KSTP–TV in 1985, he was Sports Director for WBAY–TV in Green Bay, Wisconsin. His career also includes positions as a weekend sports anchor for KCRG–TV in Cedar Rapids, Iowa, and WKBT–TV in La Crosse, Wisconsin. Joe earned his degree in Mass Communications from the University of Wisconsin–La Crosse.

27

BLOOM WHERE YOU ARE PLANTED -
KELLY BYRNES

The Habit: Bloom where you are planted.

By Kelly Byrnes – CEO of Voyage Consulting Group

Why: My mom taught me that when I was a child, and it has served me well. Blooming means you grow no matter what you are going through. When life gets hard like you don't make student council, you get a bad grade, or a friend lets you down, you can give up, get down on yourself, or you can grow from the situation. When you look for something good, you can blossom.

About Kelly: Kelly Byrnes grew up in Kansas City, Missouri, where she lives with her husband and dog. Their daughter lives in Montana with her fiancé and dog. Kelly's company helps other companies make decisions

and choices that align with their values. She also helps leaders do that too. Living by one's values in business is harder than it looks, and sometimes errors cause big mistakes that hurt employees, customers, or communities. Kelly has been doing that kind of work for nearly twenty years. She also teaches at the graduate level, authors books, speaks at businesses and conferences and leads an organization focused on living the spirit at work. When she's not working, Kelly volunteers in her community, walks Bebe, hangs out with her nieces and nephews, and cheers for a bunch of sports teams.

28

THINK BACKWARDS - MIKE WITTENSTEIN

The Habit: Think backwards.

By Mike Wittenstein – IBM eVisionary and founder of StoryMiners®

Why: The more you ask, "Why?" the more you learn. The more you ask, "Why?", the more quickly you begin to assemble your own view of the world. You know, your mental model of how things go together and affect each other.

My Uncle Sam (real name) taught me this technique when he asked me to 'reverse engineer' things that I saw in the world. Since he was in the travel business, he would ask me about transportation a lot. For example, at the airport, he would ask me, "How did that plane get here?". I would say something like "The pilot brought it here from the hangar." That wasn't enough for him. He wanted me to think not only about how the plane arrived, but how it was purchased and why, who built it and why it had the design it did, what other companies were involved in design/manufacture, and so on. Sometimes, it got tedious, but it's one of my most important work skills now.

Consciously creating your own mental model of how the world works is something each person should do for themselves—it doesn't come from lectures, learning, or best practices. I've noticed that people who curate their own mental model of the world are more positive, lead others at a higher level, and are generally happier.

ABOUT MIKE: During junior high school, Mike's most valuable lesson came not from the classroom, but from the business venture, he started on the side. That effort began to take off when he figured out how to simplify, share, and engage others with the vision that was in his head. Crafting a success story about the future appeared to be a conduit to actual success. Mike honed his storytelling skills in the businesses he founded in grad school, as well as in the two successful agencies he later started. As an eVisionary for Global Services at IBM, he created an internal incubator that birthed new consultancies while saving IBM over a billion dollars. Coming full circle, Mike founded his consultancy, StoryMiners, in

2002 to coach other business leaders in designing and implementing their own success stories. His clients were astonished at how Mike's approach cut through typical internal roadblocks to gain buy-in and traction for their initiatives. Mike also now shares his unique ideas in the keynote talks he gives around the world.

29

ASK THE DAILY QUESTION - JIM CATHCART

The Habit: Ask the Daily Question

By Jim Cathcart – Golden Gavel Award Winner, Cavett Award Winner, Author, NSA Hall of Fame Professional Speaker, Top 1% TEDx

Why: The Daily Question is, "How would the person I'd like to be do what I'm about to do?" When you think about the kind of person you want to be and consider each thing you do from the point of view, "how would that person, the better, smarter, cooler me, do what I'm about to do?" Then you move past the limits of today and the past, and you start behaving like the future you. Happy Achievers have done this for centuries. Christians ask, "What would Jesus do?" Others ask, "What would my mentor advise me to do?" When you dream of the future you, your better self, you can use him or her as your guide for how to live today more effectively. This will help you to become a person others will admire, and the "you", you will be proud to be.

 **ABOUT JIM:** Jim Cathcart is the author of 20 books, Hall of Fame professional speaker, and Top 1% TEDx speaker, Jim Cathcart has been helping people to succeed since 1976. He has delivered more than 3,200 professional speeches and seminars around the world and created a wealth of online courses, videos, international bestseller books, and more. Starting as an undereducated, overweight government clerk in his 20s, today he is one of the leading authorities in the world of motivation and achievement.

Based in Southern California, Jim plays guitar in clubs, runs mountain trails and rides his motorcycle on the best winding roads he can find. He is an example of living fully and living well while giving value to others wherever he goes.

30

COMMIT TO ONE SMALL COURAGEOUS
ACT A DAY - MANDY BASS

The Habit: Commit to one small courageous act a day

By Mandy Bass – Success Coach

Why: When you consistently stretch beyond your comfort zone to do something you otherwise would have avoided, you build your "courage muscle," resilience and self–confidence. Examples of the applying conscious courage: Make a difficult phone call, allow yourself to feel and process an emotion you would otherwise resist, ask for help, take responsibility, apologize.

Conscious courage builds a better self –image and your idea about what you are capable of, what is possible for you, and what you deserve expands automatically. As a side benefit, you do a lot of little things you might otherwise avoid, and that has a positive effect too. This simple habit naturally makes you more resilient and helps you become more successful in all areas of life.

ABOUT MANDY: For twenty years, Success Coach, Mandy Bass taught people to negotiate the turbulent waters of business and life. What she didn't realize was how important those skills would be in saving herself.

In 2016, Mandy found herself beaten, broken and almost bankrupt after she was brutally attacked during a home invasion. Against all odds, she got herself back on her feet and rebuilt her business and her life. Within six months of returning to work she grew her income from zero to 6 figures using the same sales, marketing and mindset strategies she teaches her clients.

Mandy Bass is an expert in understanding and influencing the human mind. She specializes in helping business owners develop the internal resources they need to be successful, and as importantly, get inside the mind of their target markets to improve sales, customer satisfaction and profitability.

Mandy has been featured on NBC's Today Show with Megyn Kelly and in People Magazine. She has shared the stage with Wayne Dyer, Deepak Chopra, Greg Braden and other world-famous thought leaders.

31

ALWAYS STRIVE FOR TONE - GARY GOPAR

The Habit: Always strive for tone

By Gary Gopar - Professor & Department Chair of Music, Internationally Acclaimed Trumpet Player

Why: Your personalized sound as a musician is paramount. The tone quality you create through your instrument or voice is the most important aspect of being a professional musician. Have you ever heard the saying, "find your own voice?" This could not be a truer question in the world of music and life.

Music: You can have a huge range, negotiate blistering fast tempos and have memorized thousands of songs, but without a gorgeous sound, who cares? In the bigger picture of the musical world, your "sound" is your voice and is the bottom line to everything. This should be the focus of every practice session and performance, always striving to become clearer, down the center, in-tune and more beautiful.

Life: What do you think is your voice as it pertains to your life and those that surround it? Do you even have one? Your upbringing and life experiences help shape your voice. More importantly, how you learn from getting back up after getting knocked down by life is the quickest and most effective way in finding your path to your personalized voice. This can also be characterized as your wisdom through experiences. Your voice or tone of life is special and personal to your life experiences.

Always strive for tone

About Gary: Currently chair of the music department at Cypress College, Gary Gopar has been teaching music in southern California and around the United States for twenty-two years and is Director of the Cypress College Jazz Big Band. His teaching and coaching experience include his six years at Cypress College, as well as at Long Beach City College. At the same time, Mr. Gopar is a sought-after musician who has played in a variety of settings from Long Beach Dub All-Stars to Tierra, from the Disneyland Christmas Fantasy Parade to Princess Cruises.

A Conn-Selmer CenterStage Endorsed Artist, Professor

Gopar plays on a Bb Bach Stradivarius 37S trumpet and currently holds a trumpet chair with the Arturo Sandoval Big Band. Having earned his Bachelor of Arts in Music and Master of Music in Jazz Studies from California State University, Long Beach, Mr. Gopar has traveled throughout Europe, Mexico, and the United States, playing in a wide range of styles..

32

ANCHOR IN YOUR CORE BEFORE YOUR FEET HIT THE FLOOR - DR. SUE MORTER

The Habit: Anchor in Your Core Before Your Feet Hit the Floor.

By Dr. Sue Morter – Founder of Morter Institute and Master of Bio Energetics

Why: Anchoring in the core is a way of centering in the body for higher consciousness with every move you make. In a fast–paced and hectic world that can cause our busy minds to spin, we can come "home" to ourselves by breathing deep into our belly, focusing our attention in our core and connecting with our profound truth residing there. When we do, we cultivate a sense of peace, ignite our spirit, and allow our true self to shine! Why not let the body help the mind make better decisions for your life? Anchor in your core before your feet even hit the floor! I recommend doing it 100 times a day until it ignites your new "come from" in life.

 ABOUT DR. SUE: Dr. Sue Morter is an international speaker, Master of Bioenergetic Medicine, and Quantum Field visionary. Through her seminars, retreats, presentations, and book, The Energy Codes: The 7–Step System to Awaken Your Spirit, Heal Your Body, and Live Your Best Life, Dr. Sue illuminates the relationship of quantum science and energy medicine, as well as the elevation of human consciousness and life mastery. With more than 30 years of experience as a doctor and facilitator of groups and individuals interested in natural healing and a better life, Dr. Sue shares her developments and unique perspective drawn from a life–changing awakening during ancient meditation practices. She is the co–creator of the Bio Energetic Synchronization Technique (B.E.S.T.) and founder of the Morter Institute for Bioenergetics, an organization committed to teaching individuals self–healing techniques and a new approach to life–based on Quantum Science.

33

DECIDE TO BE AWESOME EVERYDAY - ERIK SWANSON

The Habit: Decide to be AWESOME Everyday

By Erik Swanson – Author, Speaker, Habits & Attitude Success Coach

Why: If I could instill one amazing habit that I wish I knew earlier in my life, it would be the habit of deciding to be AWESOME! You literally have the choice to decide how you feel each and every day. Too many people in the world allow others to determine our feelings and attitudes during the day. How many of you are allowing others to rent space in your mind, yet you are not even charging them rent for it? Make a clear decision to be 'AWESOME' and watch your world grow in such a positive way. You have that choice!

ABOUT ERIK: As a leading Professional Speaker & Attitude Success Coach ERIK "MR AWESOME" SWANSON has been making a massive name for himself in assisting people throughout the U.S., Canada & Europe overachieve specific goals in business as well as their personal lives. He is in high demand, speaking on average to more than 50,000 people per year in various industries and careers, he is both versatile in his approach and effective in facilitating a wide array of training topics. People love to listen to him, as he shares real life experiences. He has shared the stage with some of the most talented and famous Speakers of the world today such as Brian Tracy, Jack Canfield, Les Brown, and the late great Jim Rohn. These real–life experiences have molded him into the amazing "Connector" and Speaker he is today. He is an active member of the speaking community... and the President & CEO of Habitude Warrior International providing training to corporations and individuals throughout the world! Mr. Swanson has created and developed the super popular Habitude Warrior Conference which has a 2–year waiting list and includes 33 top named speakers, all in a 'Ted Talk' style event which has quickly climbed as one of the top 10 events not to miss in the United States! Erik is honored to have spoken at the Harvard Business and Entrepreneur School as well as being invited as one of the main Keynote Speakers on the Think and Grow Rich Legacy Tour. Erik's motto is clear: "NDSO!" No Drama – Serve Others!

34

TAKE FIVE MINUTES FOR GRATITUDE AT THE BEGINNING OF YOUR DAY - MICHAEL GREGORY

The Habit: Take five minutes for gratitude at the beginning of your day

By Michael Gregory – International Speaker, Qualified Mediator and Negotiator

Why: It turns out that if we take just five minutes at the beginning of our day to reflect on what we are grateful for our brains to produce various chemicals and hormones that stay with us for up to 8 hours. This helps us have a much better perspective of ourselves, of others and our day.

Gratitude is the first pillar of the five pillars for happiness according to the class on happiness offered at Yale University. This is reinforced by the neuroscientists at the

Greater Good Science Center at the University of California at Berkeley and their analysis of gratitude. When we affirm the many gifts we have received that are outside of ourselves, and we take the time to reflect on these gifts at the beginning of our day, we enable various chemicals and hormones into our bloodstream that allows us to have a much better attitude for the day. Reflect gratitude daily at the beginning of your day, and you are far more likely to have a better day.

 **ABOUT MIKE:** Mike is an international speaker, qualified mediator, negotiator, and solution provider that helps clients overcome conflict with The Collaboration Effect®. Mike is also a student of practical applications of neuroscience

Mike has helped hundreds of clients resolve conflicts and negotiate winning solutions business to government (IRS), business to business and within businesses.

- Accredited Senior Appraiser in Business Valuation with the American Society of Appraisers
- Certified Valuation Analyst with the National Association of Certified Valuators and Analysts
- Qualified Mediator with the Minnesota Supreme Court

- Member, National Speaker's Association
- Faculty with National Speaker's Association – Speaker Academy

35

BE CURIOUS AND EXPLORE - RAY WAITE

The Habit: Be curious and explore

By Ray Waite – Futurist, Speaker, Trainer, and Founder of Lighthouse Force

Why: As a small child, there is so much wonderment in the world and so many things to learn and explore! Each and every one of us starts our life with this sense of curiosity, which leads to our learning how to walk, talk, and interact within the wonderful planet we live. But over time, we learn many rules we must follow, and we find that not everyone in charge of us appreciates our curious mind and behavior. This can lead to a dampening of our learning. I have found that as I aged, the most important thing that has kept me young at heart is to be always curious and learning. The world is quite complex today, and to stay on top of all of the amazing changes, I sometimes believe I am learning more in my fifties than I did in all my previous decades. The result of staying curious is the development of a "growth mindset" that always asks questions, is not afraid to say "I don't know," and can benefit each of us tremendously in our lives.

ABOUT RAY: Ray Waite is a futurist, passionate about helping individuals, entrepreneurs, and organizations understand and develop the skills necessary to survive in the workplace of the future. He offers a unique perspective to his speaking and training audiences by pulling on his experience as a senior corporate manager, engineer, project manager, consultant, and college adjunct instructor. Ray loves to take the complex and explain it in easy–to–understand ways that lead to quick actions and steps to improve individuals or an organization. He founded the company Lighthouse Force to help others learn the critical skills of the future: innovation, critical thinking, and design thinking,. Having raised four daughters, Ray now loves spending time with his three granddaughters, whose incredible sense of curiosity helps keeps him young and optimistic about the world.

36

MAINTAIN THE ABILITY TO QUESTION AND KEEPING YOUR CHILDLIKE WONDER AND CURIOSITY ALIVE - DR. DAIN HEER

Habit: Maintain the ability to question and keeping your childlike wonder and curiosity alive.

By Dr. Dain Heer - Energy Transformation Virtuoso, Author, International Speaker

Why: By maintaining the ability to question with and seeing the world with a childlike curiosity, you never go into judgment of yourself or others. With this mindset, you keep the awareness that the question can open the door to all the beauty of the world. The question is never a judgment, but a shining bright light that illuminates what else is out there. It helps to show you how much better something can be.

By living this way instead of judging or coming to a

conclusion, you are asking, "What is this?" "What is the adventure I can have with this?" When you do this, you open up doors to opportunity rather than close yourself in and isolate yourself from the wonderful possibilities.

Each day, take a moment and say, "If I had my childlike wonder available now, how could I look at this?". How does it get better? What else is possible. What choices are available that I have never considered before.

Being able to question with a childlike wonder and curiosity will have an incredible impact on all areas of your life.

ABOUT DAIN: Dain Heer is an internationally renowned author, speaker, and facilitator of consciousness and change. For over 17 years, he has been inviting people to embrace their true greatness—people from every culture, country, age, and social strata of society. Originally trained as a chiropractor, he has a completely different approach to healing by facilitating people to tap into and recognise their *own* abilities and knowing.

In his talks and workshops, he uses a unique set of tools and provides step by step energetic processes to get people out of the answers, conclusions and judgments that are keeping them stuck in a cycle of no choice and no change – leading them into the moments of awe that have the power to change anything.

For Dain, judgment is the biggest killer on the planet, especially the judgment of ourselves. Based on his own life experience, he asks: "What if we could get out of the wrongness of ourselves and see every wrongness, the places where judge ourselves the most, as a strongness? What would be possible then?"

Every year, Dain receives thousands of emails from readers who say that his most recent book, 'Being You Changing the World', inspired them to live. Somehow he is able to lead people out of their self-criticism and innate feeling of never being enough into a sense of question and wonder and gratitude for being alive.

Dain Heer comes from a broken family, growing up with his mother in a ghetto area of Los Angeles. During these years, he was exposed to mental, physical, emotional, sexual and monetary abuse. Everything he chose and wanted was taken from him. Very early on, he learned that he didn't own anything.

Yet, Dain never chose to be a victim. Instead he discovered the power of total allowance, courage, and resilience. He learned to transform life's challenges into a gift of strength, awareness and continuous questions. Along the way, what came forward in him was a true kindness of being, and a phenomenal knowing that has made him an agent of change rarely seen in this world.

Today he is acknowledged worldwide for his unique

perspectives on consciousness and personal transformation, that are unlike anything else out there. He is best known for his powerful energetic transformation process, called *The Energetic Synthesis of Being* and for being the co-creator of *Access Consciousness*, along with the founder, Gary Douglas.

Reaching far beyond what people say with words, Dain looks at the energy of what is being presented, inviting change at the core of each being he comes across. He invites people to truly live. To live without apology, with total presence, no longer needing to hide their differences and unique capacities from the world.

What if it is our differences embraced rather than judged and made wrong, that will bring about a greater world?

More About Dain Heer

A Doctor of Chiropractic, born and raised in California, USA, Dain Heer hosts a regular radio show entitled Conversations in Consciousness on Voice of America. He has been a guest on hundreds of nationally syndicated radio shows. He also has appeared on several TV shows including 'Fox News', 'Good Morning' Shows in New Zealand, Australia and Canada and on Gaiam TV.

Dain Heer is the author of nine books on the topics of embodiment, healing, money and relationships. *Being You, Changing the World* is now an international best seller. It was published in June 2011 and has been translated into Swedish, German, Spanish, Italian, Estonian and Japanese

37

MASH (MAKE A SMILE HAPPEN) - JOHN FLOYD

The Habit: MASH (Make A Smile Happen)

By John Floyd – Speaker, Comedian and Author

Why: Sometimes, the smallest things we do can make someone's day, or ruin it. We're all quick to complain, but how often do we go out of our way to pay someone a compliment? "You're always so well dressed." "Whenever I come here I hope you'll be the one to help me because you do such a good job." Little compliments like that can go a long way. People will stand in line for an hour just to say, "I'm never setting my foot in here again." But have you ever waited around for even five minutes just to say, "I love coming here."? Try it sometime. The smile you put on someone's face could make a massive difference in their life. Every night when you go to bed, ask yourself, "did I MASH today?".

 ABOUT JOHN: John Floyd has been traveling the world for over a quarter of a century, making people smile as a comedian and speaker. He has hit the stage over 5,000 times in front of more than two million people. Along the way, he has shared the stage with every comedian from Milton Berle to Chris Rock. He has also worked with such music acts like Frankie Valli, Chubby Checker, Michael Bolton, and Martina McBride. John says the men in his family have always been good storytellers. He's just the first one to do it on a stage instead of a front porch.

38

KEEP YOUR PROMISES - DIANNA BOOHER

The Habit: Keep your promises.

By Dianna Booher – Bestselling Author

Why: People will learn to always trust what you say. Most people have good intentions. They want to please others, be kind, and do important things. But far fewer people actually have the discipline to follow through on their word. Things become hard. Time slips by, and they feel rushed and under pressure to do other urgent things. So they leave the difficult stuff undone and do only the easy, quick things. As a result, others can never count on them to keep their promises. But if you ALWAYS keep your promises and do what you say, people will learn that they can depend on you. They will always trust you with important jobs and with the most important information.

ABOUT DIANNA: Dianna Booher is the Bestselling Author of 48 books, published in 60 foreign-language editions. She helps organizations communicate clearly and leaders to expand their influence by a strong executive presence. She has been seen in National Media such as Good Morning America, USA Today, Wall Street Journal, Investor's Business Daily, Bloomberg, Forbes, Fast Company, FOX, CNN, NPR, Success, and Entrepreneur have interviewed her on workplace communication issues.

39

DON'T TRY TO BE THE BEST YOU CAN BE. JUST BE THE BEST YOU'VE EVER BEEN - ALAN BERG

Habit: Don't try to be the best you can be. Just be the best you've ever been

By Alan Berg – CSP, Global Speaking Fellow

Why: Don't seek perfection, it's a fool's game. Besides being almost impossible to achieve, I believe it's a wrong goal because you can't improve upon perfection. What keeps me going is always knowing that I can be better, do better, act better, whether it's personally or professionally. If you play a sport, try to be better each game or match. If you're studying in school, try to learn something new every day. If you're plying a craft, or working a job, try to be better, every time. Every time I give a speech, I want it to be the best I've ever given. But, I never want it to be the best I can ever give, or it will be the last I ever give. It's knowing that you're always improving, no matter how skilled you already are, that makes every day a fun challenge.

 **ABOUT ALAN:** Alan Berg has been called "the Leading Speaker and Expert on the Business of Weddings and Events." He's a Certified Speaking Professional® and one of only 33 Global Speaking Fellows in the world. After publishing two wedding magazines, Alan spent 11 years at The Knot and he's now an education guru for WeddingWire, the leading wedding technology company. He's presented in twelve countries, four of them in Spanish, and he's the author of 4 books: "If your website was an employee, would you fire it?", "Your Attitude for Success," "Shut Up and Sell More Weddings & Events," and "Why Don't They Call Me? 8 tips for converting wedding & event inquiries into sales."

40

LOVE YOURSELF, NO MATTER WHAT - THERESA PUSKAR

The Habit: Love yourself, no matter what

By Theresa Puskar – Speaker, Entertainer and Author

Why: You have been brought up in a world where you are told that Santa only leaves gifts when you are nice, where you are often told that you are "bad" when you make a mistake. You are never bad. You are awesome! While sometimes you make bad choices, you are trying your best, even when you make mistakes. If you knew better, you would have behaved differently. It is so important that you love yourself, no matter what! When you treat others unkindly, you do so because you don't accept yourself. For a moment, you feel good and powerful, but afterwards, you like yourself less. When you are unkind to someone, take a moment and send yourself a lot of love and forgiveness. Then you feel better about yourself, and when you do, you are more apt to apologize and be kinder to others. Also, when others bully you, remember – it's not about anything you did or didn't do. It's about the bully feeling weak and bad about him or herself.

ABOUT THERESA: AS A TRANSFORMATION LEADER, "TRUE" power Speaker, Entertainer, and Author, Theresa Puskar has had the privilege of spreading her own unique kind of inspiration throughout the continent. As the founder of Edu–Tainment Productions, she is passionate about educating, while entertainment her clients and audiences alike. Whether serving as a transformation leader through providing keynote speaking, corporate coaching or training to Fortune 500 companies, healing through inspirational or motivational speaking, officiating spiritual gatherings, serving as a television/radio host, or performing her one–woman show, she weaves profound and often hilarious storytelling into all that she does. Best known for her authenticity and unique ability to stir the hearts and minds of those with whom she engages, her refreshing and heartfelt "tell it like it is" approach to edu–taining is not to be missed!

41

WITH EVERYONE YOU INTERACT WITH, LEARN WHAT THEY ARE INTERESTED IN - ART SOBCZAK

The Habit: With everyone you interact with, learn what they are interested in.

By Art Sobczak – Author, Speaker, Sales Trainer

Why: This is the foundation for success in virtually every aspect of life. Almost everything you want is owned or controlled by someone else. The very best way to get someone to do something is showing them or helping them get what they want. It is the basis for professional sales, great personal and business relationships, brightening the lives of others, and being charismatic and attractive to them. Ask questions, genuinely listen, be curious and interested, and you will see more abundance coming back to you.

 **About Art:** For over 30 years Art Sobczak has helped sales professionals––and those who might not have "sales" in the title but still must sell–– say the right things to prospect and sell conversationally, without "rejection." He has done over 1500 training programs, ranging from keynotes to multi–day sales workshops. His award–winning book, "Smart Calling––Eliminate the Fear, Failure, and Rejection from Cold Calling" is the standard for companies and individuals worldwide as the effective alternative to "cold" calling. He received the Lifetime Achievement Award from the American Association of Inside Sales Professionals.

42

ONCE A QUARTER, WRITE DOWN TEN EXAMPLES OF WHAT YOU CAN'T DO VERY WELL - BRENT SCARPO

The Habit: Once a quarter, write down ten examples of what you can't do very well, your ten weaknesses.

By Brent Scarpo – Speaker, Life Coach, Producer, Writer, Director

Why: We are so GOOD at writing down our strengths, what we are GREAT at in terms of our skills, but rarely do we take inventory of what we are NOT good at doing, our weaknesses, what we can't stand doing in our lives. I give this assignment to my clients all the time and then offer the following choices:

- Take classes or educate yourself on those items that need improving.
- Hire someone to take over those responsibilities

to give you more time to do what you are good at doing.

- If this is business related, find an expert in your office, who excels in what you would rather not do and delegate the job.

About Brent: Brent Scarpo has over thirty years of experience as a national speaker, life coach, producer, writer, director, and casting director in Hollywood. He has worked on such well-known films as THE SHAWSHANK REDEMPTION, THAT THING YOU DO, AIRFORCE ONE and MATILDA. Additionally, Brent has presented thousands of programs to high schools, colleges, and corporate America numbering well over one million participants.

Scarpo wrote and was featured on the Christmas Special, CHRISTMAS MIRACLES for ABC and recently won The Today Show's writing contest, EVERYONE HAS A STORY where his story, THE RED BALLOON was chosen out of 100,000 entries. It was one of The Today's Shows top stories and Kathy Lee Gifford said, "This was our favorite story and we saved the best for last." Scarpo is currently writing his book, THE RED BALLOON AND OTHER INSPIRATIONAL STORIES and continues to speak around the world, where he has enjoyed presenting in each state as well as numerous foreign countries.

43

TAKE RESPONSIBILITY FOR YOUR
MISTAKES - BILL JELEN

The Habit: Take responsibility for your mistakes.

By Bill Jelen – Founder of MrExcel Publishing

Why: No one is perfect. Everyone will make a mistake now and then. When you make a mistake, stand up and admit that you made a mistake, you've learned from the mistake, and you will avoid making the same mistake again. Others will respect that you know and admit your mistake. They will respect you far more than the person who never takes responsibility and always blames their mistakes on someone else.

About Bill: Online, he's known as MrExcel, but offline, he's better known as Bill Jelen, a real-life Excel expert. Bill has over 29 years of spreadsheet experience. He has been doing Excel consulting since 1998, Excel speaking

since 2002, and has written over 40 books about Excel.

Bill travels the world, delivering his entertaining and informative Power Excel seminar to people who use Excel. He makes sure that everyone goes home with new tricks and one of his best-selling books to reinforce the techniques taught in the seminar. However, Bill's seminars are interactive and he encourages his audience to "show him up" by providing faster ways to solve Excel problems. The seminar that Bill delivers today is better thanks to many tricks offered from "Row 2" over the years.

Bill wrote his first book, Guerilla Data Analysis in 2002. Since then, he has authored 43 books, including Pivot Table Data Crunching, Excel Gurus Gone Wild, Don't Fear the Spreadsheet, and Power Pivot Alchemy. He started a small press, publishing works by other Excel MVPs such as Bob Umlas, Mike Girvin, Rob Collie, Chris Smith, and Zack Barresse.

44

NEVER STOP LEARNING - MOHAMED TOHAMI

The Habit: Never stop learning

By Mohamed Tohami – Bestselling Author and Entrepreneur

Why: My mentor, Jim Cathcart, was always telling me, "Tohami, you are like a sponge. Your appetite for continuous learning and improvement will take you very far."

What makes me always hungry for learning is that I believe that you're one idea away from your next breakthrough.

That's why if you would choose only ONE habit to be ultra successful, it should be non–stop learning. It doesn't matter what level of success you've reached, one new book can take you to a whole new level.

Whenever I feel that my personal or business growth curve has reached a plateau, I immediately start searching for a new book, course or seminar to learn something new ... something powerful.

And it goes without saying, learning without applying is the ultimate waste of life. That's why I commit myself to implement at least ONE idea from every book or course I take.

If you read one book per month, that's applying 12 new powerful ideas every year that makes you more successful.

I never stop learning. It is the ONLY thing I know and can't recommend enough that guarantees everlasting success.

 **ABOUT MOHAMED:** Mohamed Tohami is the Chief Dreamer and Founder of The Passion Point. He is on a mission to transform the state of unfulfilled employees worldwide. Tohami is a Bestselling Author and creator of the Passion To Profit SystemTM. It is the world's easiest & safest system to help you quit your unfulfilling job and turn your passion into a profitable business.

45

MEDITATE EVERYDAY - DR. HASSAN TETTEH

The Habit: Meditate Everyday

By Dr. Hassan Tetteh – Heart and Lung Transplant Surgeon

Why: You become the best version of yourself through meditation. When you take the time to meditate in the silence and listen to the still quiet voice within, you begin to become truly great. Through meditation, you also achieve the "H.E.H. effect." Daily meditation yields the following three benefits: · Health · Effectiveness · Happiness Meditation is proven to lower stress, high blood pressure, and depression, and this can lead to improved health. With improved health, you become more effective in your relationships, at work, and in life. When you are healthy and effective in all the things you are meant to do, you move closer to realizing your real purpose in life, and this ultimately leads to happiness.

ABOUT DR. TETTEH: Dr. Hassan Tetteh is an experienced Physician Executive and Thoracic Surgeon. He is triple–board certified in surgery, thoracic surgery, and clinical informatics specialties. Dr. Tetteh is an expert in heart health, heart and lung transplantation, informatics, and compassionate health care delivery and Savoy magazine recognized his clinical leadership and named Tetteh a 'Hero of Medicine' for his Specialized Thoracic Adapted Recovery (STAR) Team, based in Washington, D.C. His research in thoracic transplantation aims to expand heart and lung organ recovery nationwide and save lives.

46

GET WORK ROUGHLY DONE WAY AHEAD OF THE DUE DATE AND REFINE OVER TIME - ROBERT T. WHIPPLE

The Habit: Get work roughly done way ahead of the due date and refine over time

By Robert T. Whipple – Top 100 Leadership Speakers by Inc. Magazine

Why: It reduces the time pressure, which improves the quality of your work and reduces your stress level. It gives you time to think of other exciting angles to enhance the product. You are never late and are not always stressing about not enough time to get things done. There is time to check out your ideas with others before the work goes out. Because you are prepared ahead of time, you are more self–confident in your product and presentation. It takes some discipline to get in the habit of operating ahead of the power curve, but it makes a massive difference in the quality of your work and your frame of mind.

 **About Bob:** Known internationally as "The Trust Ambassador," Bob Whipple teaches leaders and organizations the value of higher trust and how to obtain it, maintain it, and repair it. A corporate leader for over 30 years and now an Independent Consultant, Author, Teacher, and Coach, Bob has published four books on the topic of building higher trust in organizations. He has been named as a "Lifetime Achievement Award Winner" as a top thought leader in trust by Trust Across America: Trust Around the World. He has been named as one of the top 100 Leadership Speakers by Inc. Magazine for the past three years. He was also named one of the top 15 thought leaders on leadership by Leadership Excellence Magazine. Bob has published over 650 articles on leadership and trust, and he has made over 100 videos on all aspects of leadership. He the Chairman of the Board of Directors of the Rochester Area Business Ethics Foundation RABEF. He is a member of the National Speakers Association and the National Human Resource Association. He is also a member of the Greater Rochester Chamber of Commerce, Rochester Rotary, and the Rochester Chapter of Conscious Capitalism.

47

CONSTANTLY SHARE REMINDERS AND ENCOURAGEMENT - SEAN GLAZE

The Habit: Share Reminders and Encouragement

By Sean Glaze – Author and Speaker

Why: Having coached basketball for over 20 years, one of the best things I could say about a person is that he or she is a great teammate. Players who may not have been blessed with size or speed or height or agility were still able to have a substantial positive impact on our team by being a great teammate. That same effort and positive attitude is something that people in your industry can contribute to your team, regardless of skills or specific abilities. Being a great teammate means you are constantly thinking, "what does the TEAM need?" and acting accordingly. That is why sharing reminders and encouragements is one of the 10 Commandments of Winning Teammates–

and the 1 habit I would enthusiastically encourage people to adopt.

Reminders are evidence that you have taken the initiative to think ahead and to influence others to do what the team needs. Instead of waiting until after a mistake is made, great teammates share reminders to inspire people around them to stay focused and successfully take care of the things that the team needs from them. An encouraging reminder is a powerful way to keep common issues from occurring.

 **About Sean:** Sean Glaze is an Author, Engaging Speaker, and fun Team Building Facilitator who inspires groups to have fun laughing together so they can have more success working together. His three books are powerful parables for building and leading great teams! As a successful basketball coach and educator for over 20 years, Sean gained valuable insights into how to develop winning teams – and founded Great Results Teambuilding to share those lessons... Sean is a member of both the South East Association of Facilitators and the National Speakers Association, where he earned the distinction of "Member of the Year" for 2015.

48

EMBODY THE MESSAGE YOU WISH TO IMPART - JEFF DAVIDSON

The Habit: Embody the message you wish to impart

By Jeff Davidson – *The Work–Life Balance Expert®*

Why: It's not necessary to walk your talk every minute of the day to influence others. There are ways to embody the message you want to impart so that others get your message by merely being in your presence. Personally, I choose to embody the Breathing Space principles. Here's what that means to me:

- Not wearing a watch. If I have meetings, I ensure that I'm near a timepiece.
- Pausing several times a day for one minute to collect my thoughts and breathe deeply.
- Doing one thing at a time. For example, I don't

eat while I read, doodle while I talk on the
phone, or give divided attention in conversation
with others.

So, to embody the message that you wish to impart to
others, what personal attributes and traits can you
develop or improve?

 **About Jeff:** Jeff Davidson, the *Work
Life Balance Expert®*, can move an
audience like few others. Jeff offers
dynamic learning keynotes and
seminar presentations. He combines
outstanding content with humor,
flair, and inspiration to help listeners manage information and communication overload. Jeff supercharges his
audiences to master their to-do lists, manage interrup-
tions, and take action.

Frequently quoted or featured in *USA Today,* the *New
York Times, The Washington Post, Chicago Tribune,* and the
Los Angeles Times; in *Fortune, Forbes,* and *Businessweek*; and
on 175 talk shows.

Jeff is the past president of the NSA Carolinas Chapter
and former national chair of the Public Relations
Committee of the Institute of Management Consultants.
He has also been a member of the board of directors of
Washington Independent Writers, and for five years
running, won the U.S. Small Business Administration's
state "Media Advocate of the Year."

49

NEVER STOP TAKING ACTION AND PATIENTLY ENDURE THE PROCESS. - DIANA MAUX

Habit: Never stop taking action and patiently endure the process

By Diana Maux - Holistic Fitness Coach

Why: It takes action to build the results we want in any aspect of our life and career, and the only way to achieve progress is through action. When we learn the skill of balancing action and patience, your personal and professional growth will be unstoppable and most importantly, enjoyable.

Patience is imperative for better mental health but still an overlooked virtue; especially; in today's world, where instant gratification and getting what we want instantaneously have become part of our newest generation's culture.

So just remember, no need to worry. Just never stop taking action and be patient. But your action has to come from the heart, not from the ego; otherwise, it will only generate anxiety and stress. There is no reason to rush, you are not going to take money, tittles, or anything with you to the grave.

When you take action, regardless of the final result, you will let go of expectations. Do this will help you to start living a more positive life, enjoying the present, and best of all, action will flow naturally as your breath.

> **"Live your passions by taking action, and tame your passions by being patient."**

About Diana: Straight out of Colombia! Diana Maux was an overweight child and walked around with a target on her back! The constant bullying made her very shy, which led to suffering from eating disorders. However, rough childhood fueled her and built her foundation to help others.

Through her fitness journey, she has developed Maux Training, where she combined her knowledge in different physical disciplines to transform lives along the way. She strives to share her vision and knowledge of fitness with others, and with her Latino community in the USA. She continues focusing on a holistic fitness approach, developing a better self and improving the quality of life from within - Unconditional Self Love, Nutrition and Training.

She is also part of an ONG foundation "Mamachama" for the development and empowerment of women in vulnerable communities, that have been affected by violence in her home country Colombia.

50

ASSUME POSITIVE INTENT - MERRICK ROSENBERG

The Habit: Assume positive intent

By Merrick Rosenberg – Bestselling Author

Why: Throughout your life, people will do things that you think are disrespectful. If you assume that they were purposely trying to hurt you, they will make you angry, and you will give your power away to them. Never give others the power to control your emotions. Instead, recognize that each of us is just doing our best to get by and meet our own needs. Remain calm and hold firm to the belief that others are not thinking about your needs, they are thinking of their own. Don't get mad about that, because it's really not about you. It's about them trying to do the best they can to get what they want. Give others the benefit of the doubt and instead of assuming they are intentionally being mean, assume that they mean well.

 **About Merrick:** Merrick Rosenberg co–founded Team Builders Plus, one of the first team building companies, in 1991 and Take Flight Learning in 2012. He is the author of The Chameleon and Taking Flight!, two books about personality styles. Under Merrick's leadership, his company has been selected as the New Jersey Business of the Year and named one of the Fastest Growing Companies and Best Places to Work in the Philadelphia area a combined 14 times over the past 11 years. He received his MBA from Drexel University who recognized him as the Alumni Entrepreneur of the Year. Merrick has worked with more than two–thirds of the Fortune 100 companies in the US and around the world and has spoken to hundreds of thousands of people about teamwork, leadership, and driving success.

51

TEACH - MARK LEVIT

The Habit: Teach

By Mark Levit – Founder of the Citizen Professor
Institute

Why: Employers and HR executives have labeled the current generation of college graduates "not ready for the workplace." That's despite these young degreed people being part if the most educated generation in history.

Fact is, a university's purpose is not to provide skills training for the workplace. A university's job is to educate, to provide "academic rigor" to help students to think more clearly.

Boomers didn't have workplace skills when they entered the workforce, employers mentored their new hires and offered training programs. Budgets today don't allow for such training, but executives can connect with local universities and provide themselves as guest speakers, to teach as adjuncts, or offer to mentor students.

Executives can invite students to intern for their organizations and instead of requiring them to file papers, fetch coffee, or "do some of that social media stuff," they can teach what they want new hires to know about their businesses and the commercial sector.

It feels good to teach, teaching is good for the nation's growth, and it can even help employers discover and nurture their next "superstar" employees.

 **ABOUT MARK:** Mark Levit has been a New York advertising agency principal, Internet pioneer, commercial voiceover, a caregiver, a mentor, and a university professor. He's the founder of the Citizen Professor Institute, a movement dedicated to aligning the expectations of employers with those of college students and recent graduates. Mark began working in education in 1995 at New York University and teaches currently at the University of Miami. He is also a regular guest instructor at the Hofstra University Graduate School of Healthcare Marketing's Intensive MBA for Physicians Program.

52

FEED YOUR BODY WITH THE RIGHT FUEL - ROBIN HOFFMAN HAACK

The Habit: Feed your body with the right fuel

By Robin Hoffman Haack – Founder and CEO of Clar8ty

Why: It's not just your parents being awful adults and nagging you when they say, "Eat your vegetables!" This tiny phrase is packed full of meaning and love. Your body deserves nothing but the best so put in the effort while you are young to feed your body with foods and drinks that bless it. A busy schedule tends to encourage us to grab the quick & easy options that are full of sugar and man-made ingredients. Your body will thank you with a lifetime of abundant health if you opt for the natural stuff now! If you bought a brand new car, you would devote extra care and money to put the highest quality fuel in the tank, so it runs for a long time. Your body is the car that will drive you through your entire life---it requires proper nutrition and gas to be full of health and last a long time. The habit of eating foods that bless your body and drinking lots of water will result in a healthy life.

ABOUT ROBIN: Building a company with a foundation in personal growth and health was a natural choice for Robin Hoffman Haack. Born into a family of entrepreneurs and world-class athletes, Robin has reached for the stars for both health and business success. The Hoffman family business is its 95th year, and every single generation of the Hoffman family has reached elite levels in the sports of surfing, swimming or horseback riding. Robin and her husband are both members of the National Cutting Horse Association Hall of Fame, and their roots in the competition have helped shape their lives and company today. Robin's drive and entrepreneurial spirit, as well as her lifelong dedication to overall health and well-being, led her to create Clar8ty.

Clar8ty is the result of one big dream and the culmination of Robin's diverse life experiences in business and sports. Robin embarked on a mission to launch an innovative company offering healthier solutions for today's fast-pace lifestyles all while offering a financial opportunity that appeals to every-day families seeking greater financial freedom. Clar8ty is the product of her dream, and has become far more than a nutritional company. It's a company dedicated to providing others with a path toward achieving their highest aspirations in all areas of life.

53

EACH DAY, WRITE DOWN 1-2 THINGS MY FUTURE SELF CAN THANK ME FOR - KRISTIN SMITH

The Habit: Each day, Write down 1-2 things my future self can thank me for

By Kristin Smith: Life & Business Strategist, Author & Podcaster

Why: It can be as simple as getting all of the housework done before I leave for the day so that when I get home, I am very thankful I did. Or it can be something more long term such as retraining, adding skills, or making solid sound connections. The point you do not want to miss here is that this particular habit can keep you in motion without losing the much-needed mojo you need in daily life. When we lose our momentum, we set ourselves up for future regret, so honor your future by working towards it daily voluntarily.

About Kristin: As a leader in business for over 18 years, Kristin Smith is a natural mover and shaker who continually sought ways to challenge and improve herself. However, when she first began her search for success and self-actualization, she found very few resources to effectively empower such a driven, positive, and motivated person.

When asked in life coaching school to identify her target market, she always pointed to herself. More interested in expanding her horizons than pursuing one particular path, Kristin found many of the coaching theories and concepts to be unclear and non-applicable to her personal journey and professional life strategy. It was only through making mistakes and overcoming the obstacles unique to a multi-linear path that she began to define her own concepts and develop her coaching curricula.

While she endorsed some popular disciplines, she found herself rejecting others to seek a better-defined and more applicable strategy for herself and highly motivated people like her. Kristin has been in business and education for over 18 years, is an award-winning leader, a mother of two fabulous children and continues to seek ways to improve self while leading others.

54

SPEAK UP - JILL CHRISTENSEN

The Habit: Speak Up

By Jill Christensen – Bestselling Author and Keynote Speaker

Why: You have a voice that deserves and needs to be heard. When you speak up – be it to share an idea, question, thought, observation, or concern -- the world benefits as only you have your unique perspective. When you sit in silence, you rob the world of your amazing creativity and curiosity. Also, remaining silent encourages others to do the same.

Be the role model: speak your mind, and you will convey confidence, knowledge, and courage, and potentially even inspire others to follow suit.

ABOUT JILL: Jill Christensen is a former Fortune 500 business executive, who led Global Internal Communications at both Avaya and Western Union. She is a Bestselling Author, International Keynote Speaker, and holds a Six Sigma Green Belt. Jill was named a Top 100 Global Employee Engagement Influencer, and partners with the best and brightest leaders around the world to improve productivity, retention, customer satisfaction, and revenue growth by re–engaging employees.

Jill has worked in 15 industries, and her proven approach to increase employee engagement has led her to speak throughout the United States, Canada, United Kingdom, Malaysia, Singapore, and India. Jill grew up in multiple U.S. states, but now calls Denver, CO, her home thanks to the incredible mountains and skiing, and her love of U.S. football and live music.

55

GET CLEAR ON WHAT WINNING IS TO YOU, IN EVERY WAY, EVERY DAY - HOLLY G. GREEN

The Habit: Get clear on what winning is to you, in every way, every day.

By Holly G. Green – Founder of The Human Factor, Inc.

Why: When you are clear on what you want/what you believe is the 'win' in any situation, you push the 'prove yourself right' button in your brain. One of our deepest instincts is to win, and one of our most profound ways of being is to prove ourselves right. Combining these two very powerful underlying prompts helps us to see possibilities and alternatives on how to achieve what we desire. It also helps to get others in the same game with us. When we can use language that frames what we want vs. what we don't want, it is a much more positive and compelling approach.

 **ABOUT HOLLY;** Holly founded The Human Factor, Inc. after working for years for some of the world's best companies. She was fascinated by the behaviors she witnessed at work and wondered why what we learn in Management 101 books are far from the actual experiences that take place in offices. She began her post–graduate studies in neurophysiology to better understand the science of thinking at work. Since then, Holly has had the privilege and the pleasure of working with elite players in many fields, including the military, athletes, musicians, and business people. She is passionate about guiding high performers and organizations in achieving greater success by teaching how to leverage your brain and the brains of others at work.

56

ALWAYS TRUST YOUR INTUITION – YOUR GUT FEELINGS - CHRIS WARNER

The Habit: Always trust your intuition – your gut feelings

By Chris Warner – Actor, Writer, Director, Producer, Voiceover Artist

Why: Its hands down, the most honest, true, and exact you'll ever get to making the best possible choice when it comes to life's difficult decisions. I like to think of my intuition as a whisper from God himself as confirmation that I'm moving in the right direction. Answers to life's questions will never be black–and–white and never easy, but they'll always be straightforward – we've just got to listen to our gut. Life's challenges are made to be difficult to help us learn work ethic, develop discipline, and ultimately have a more profound satisfaction & greater appreciation for what we've had to overcome to reach achievement. If life's taught me anything, it's that listening to my intuition is one of the most valuable, decision–making tools I've ever had to use. It's never let me down... .not once.

 **ABOUT CHRIS:** Chris Warner has been described as the kid in the candy store meets the bull in the china shop. He's kinda like if The Hulk and Winnie The Pooh were the Wonder Twins: Shape of a lovable teddy bear, Form of A big, aggressive, undeniable personality! From the second you meet him, you instantly realize that there's no doubt he was born to entertain. Armed with an intense wit and a commanding presence, he's sure to immediately grab your attention, so hold on tight!

Chris began acting professionally over two decades ago in Austin, TX. After some marked success in film, television, and commercials, Chris' last role while still living in Texas before departing for the bright lights of Hollywood, was opposite Academy Award winner Kevin Spacey in The Life of David Gale. You may also recognize him opposite Tommy Lee Jones in the Academy Award–winning film No Country for Old Men or with Benicio Del Toro's Jackie Boy in the ground–breaking movie Frank Miller's Sin City. In addition to his successful movie roles, you might have also seen him on the television shows Prison Break, Criminal Minds, Friday Night

Lights, The Event, NCIS: Los Angeles, Justified and Shut Eye.

As one of the most respected character actors of his generation, Chris has cemented himself as an edgy, intense artist who leaves nothing to chance when he appears on-screen. When he's not sharpening his acting chops or banging away at a keyboard on his next storied adventure, he can be found spending time with his queen at the beach, helping to rescue animals-in-need, supporting his beloved Texas Longhorns and leading his mission-driven clothing brand My Life Is War.

57

DO EXACTLY WHAT YOU LOVE DOING EVERYDAY - MOTOE HAUS

The Habit: Do exactly what you love doing, everyday

By Motoe Haus – Techno Music Producer and International DJ, Author

Why: I believe that this is how you become a true master of anything and everything. It's what creates real talent and success in every one of us. To do what you love, will enable you to put all your efforts towards an always inspired life. This is the recipe for greatness. The ingredient for infinite legacy and effect on the entire world.

About Motoe: As an accomplished techno producer and DJ, he has been ripping up dance floors in Ibiza from Heart as the headline resident DJ for Submission, Social at Boutique Hostal Salinas, played alongside Nick

 Warren for The Soundgarden events, Zoo Project, Monochrome Mountain, Acid Sundays and many more. His approach is free, honest, and yet structured with a workflow that is only deciphered from 45,000 hours in the studio logged over many years producing his original releases and official remixes for artists Kool n tha Gang, Jimi Hendrix, NIN, Fleetwood Mac, Jefferson Airplane, Jerome Sydenham, Samy Jarrar, SIR, Jaime Narvaez, and many more. Signed to more than 27 labels and with over 290 releases in just dance music, Motoe Haus possess an endless creative output & flow that is second to none. With ongoing weekly radio shows on Ibiza Live Radio & WhiteFM, as well as guest sets on All About the Music, Frisky Radio, Ibiza Global Radio and many others worldwide.

58

ALWAYS AIM TO EXCEED YOUR OWN AND OTHERS EXPECTATIONS - STEVE BECKLES-EBUSUA

The Habit: Always aim to exceed your own and others expectations.

By Steve Beckles–Ebusua – International Speaker, Trainer, Presenter, and Amazon Top 10 Best Seller

Why: Many of us have heard people say of individuals and organizations that their expectations were not met. On initially hearing this I used to think that's very difficult because how do we know what their expectations were? The answer, ask questions.

I wished I had listened more and then asked questions more when I was younger. I was always told we have two ears and one mouth for a reason, but I didn't understand what it meant.

Listening and then asking questions helps give you a greater understanding and trust from others.

Never forget is 'Listening builds trust.'

Andrew Carnegie was a Scottish–American industrialist, business magnate, and philanthropist who once said, "Successful people do not talk, they ask questions."

It's essential to ask questions and find out people's expectations.

You may not always be able to exceed people's expectations; however, there is no excuse for not exceeding yours.

ABOUT STEVE: In England, The Times Newspaper called him "The man with the orange tie bursting with energy and radiating self–belief." Steve is an International Speaker, Trainer, Presenter, and Amazon Top 10 bestseller. He has spoken in the USA and throughout Europe on beliefs and overcoming self–defeating habits.

Steve has more than 20 years' experience gained in speaking and training on being a formidable public speaker, developing a growth mindset, being motivated to succeed, and understanding teenagers. He has written and published books on all of these topics. He is an international speaker, trainer, and presenter; skilled in employing clarity, innovation, and humor to deliver effective presentations and workshops throughout the UK, Europe, and the USA.

The Speaker with the Orange Tie helps people to conquer lifelong self–defeating habits that hold us back from reaching our full potential. He has works with individuals and organizations to help them develop greater focus and direction in their lives and businesses.

Steve has more than 20 years' experience gained in speaking and training on being a formidable public speaker, developing a growth mindset, being motivated to succeed, and understanding teenagers. He has written and published books on all of these topics. He is an international speaker, trainer, and presenter; skilled in employing clarity, innovation, and humor to deliver effective presentations and workshops throughout the UK, Europe, and the USA.

The Speaker with the Orange Tie helps people to conquer lifelong self–defeating habits that hold us back from reaching our full potential. He has works with individuals and organizations to help them develop greater focus and direction in their lives and businesses.

59

WRITE A BOOK AND BECOME THE AUTHORITY™ - RAYMOND HARLALL

The Habit: Write a book and become the AUTHORity™

By Raymond Harlall - Founder of The Power of Collaboration Movement

Why: People do business with people they Know, Like, and Trust. When I met Bob Proctor for the first time, he said to me; "Raymond you need to write a book." He also said, "a book acts as a salesperson, working 24/7 on your behalf."

A year later I have 4 published books. This habit is universal, we all have a special gift and talent. It's a matter of packaging and promoting your narrative. Writing a book will not just make you an author but a sought-after subject matter authority.

The best part is, your book becomes your intellectual property, earning royalties over and over for life + 70 more years! There is no better way to leave a legacy.

 ABOUT RAYMOND: World Civility Ambassador, Raymond Harlall, is a speaker, entrepreneur, consultant, philanthropist who uses relationship capital to bridge the gap between, governments, non-government organizations, and local at-risk community leaders to empower young entrepreneurs in developing countries with his global initiative called iEmpower Entrepreneurs™.

Raymond is a Contributor to "The Handbook to Holistic Health H3 – A Self-help Guide to Live HAPPY, HEALTHY and WEALTHY" and a recipient of the 2018 Global Authors Award. Raymond speaks globally sharing stages with renowned speakers like Brian Tracy, Les Brown, Kevin Harrington, and Jack Canfield.

He's president of Local Experts Group, a Canadian company publishing collaborative non-fiction books, the founder of Canada Book Club creating a platform to promote authors, and producer of The Power of Collaboration, an annual world-class business and professional summit in Toronto, Canada.

He helps people brand themselves as experts using his AUTHORity™ program.   Raymond does keynote speeches globally on "How to Build Your Credibility" by being a published author, a professional speaker, and a sought-after mentor.

As a YouTuber with 2.2 million+ views in 224 countries, Raymond teaches "How to Become More Visible" through effective Video Marketing.

60

DON'T TAKE THINGS PERSONALLY - LISA BRAITHWAITE

The Habit: Don't take things personally

By Lisa Braithwaite – Speaking Coach and Author

Why: We often overreact to situations that have nothing to do with us. A friend doesn't call for two weeks, and you think you've done something to upset her. Nope, she was just busy! An audience member frowns all the way through your presentation, and you feel like you're doing a lousy job. Nope, that's just his natural facial expression! And after the presentation, he comes to tell you how much he enjoyed it. Our personal experience doesn't always reflect others' experiences. Stay open to the possibility that it's not actually about you, and that others are often wrapped up in their own worlds and experiences.

 **About Lisa:** Lisa Braithwaite is a public speaking coach, trainer, and author of the book "Presenting for Humans: Insights for Speakers on Ditching Perfection and Creating Connection." She mentors entrepreneurs and professionals to create memorable and engaging presentations so they can grow their organizations through speaking.

Before launching her business in 2005, she spent sixteen years developing and managing programs for nonprofit organizations as an advocate and educator, as well as founding her own nonprofit organization.

She has a B.A. in Theater and an M.A. in Education, and has been interviewed for the Wall Street Journal, Los Angeles Times, Chicago Tribune, Men's Health, Toastmaster Magazine, and Inc.com.

She provides training for companies as diverse as Microsoft, The National Oceanic and Atmospheric Administration, Pulmonary Fibrosis Foundation, Massachusetts Association of Realtors®, and AgWest Commodities.

Lisa's philosophy is that public speaking is fun, it's an awesome way to express yourself creatively, and it offers an accelerated approach to developing an intimate and trusting relationship with your target audience.

61

THE HABIT OF STOPPING - MARC GRIFFITHS

The Habit: The Habit of Stopping

By Marc Griffiths – Motivational Speaker and Author

Why: Because most people are too busy. They are frantically striving. They believe the lie that when they get the break, or when they win the money, or when they own the big house, that then they'll be happy. But happiness is never in the future. It's always in the now, and today's now becomes tomorrows memories, which ultimately add up to a fulfilled life. Your happiness is free, but your dreams are not. They cost. Your dreams and goals pull you forwards and bring you hope and meaning. So while you strive to achieve them, remember to develop the habit of stopping. Look at the sky. Take a breath. Be thankful in the moment. Develop the habit of stopping. It's where happiness is found. It's always a choice, and it's always in the now.

ABOUT MARC: Marc Griffiths is the Founder of 'Get Out Your Box. He is a Motivational Speaker, hilarious Ventriloquist, Author, Influencer, an expert on happiness and true success. He loves inspiring people to 'get out their box' and live incredible lives. His messages address two of the biggest problems in the world today, 'Who am I?' and 'What's my purpose?' Marc has spoken in over 5000 venues to more than 1 million people and has won multiple national awards, including a life–changing experience on Britain's Got Talent. Originally from the UK, he now lives in the States with his wife, five children, and his speaking puppet team!

62

MAKE AND KEEP YOUR PROMISE - JASON HEWLETT

The Habit: Make and Keep Your Promise

By Jason Hewlett – CSP, CPAE, Speaker Hall of Fame, Author and Leadership Expert

Why: Have you ever set a Goal and missed it? You just set a new Goal. But what about making a Promise? If you break it, you have a problem. I like to say, "Why set a Goal when we can make a Promise?" A Promise is the highest level of engagement we commit to in any experience. Stronger than a Goal, more powerful than a commitment. No man ever stood at the wedding, making his vows and said, "I set a Goal to be faithful..." It's in our Promise making and Keeping, as a Habit, that makes all the difference.

ABOUT JASON: Husband to Tami, of viral Facebook fame, following "post read around the world" by over 100 Million viewers of Jason's proclamation of love after seeing her at Target in the grocery line; proud parents of 4, family on a mission to help entrepreneurs, leaders, and families make and keep Promises to one another. Jason began his career with the Las Vegas "Legends in Concert" as a Ricky Martin and Elton John impersonator, eventually turning away headlining opportunities on The Strip in order to keep his Promise, and creating a one–man show of comedy, impressions and family–friendly entertainment for corporate events and front line fighters in the US Military in war zone Afghanistan. Building a multi–million dollar business as an award–winning entertainer and becoming one of the most sought after Keynote Speakers in the Leadership market, inducted by his peers as one of the youngest ever in the National Speakers Association Hall of Fame, Jason Hewlett is the messenger of The Promise.

63

ALWAYS EMBRACE YOUR UNIQUENESS - GAIL RUBIN

The Habit: Always embrace your uniqueness

By Gail Rubin – Certified Thanatologist

Why: Your unique characteristics often emerge when you are a child. However, to fit in and feel like we belong in a group, we may suppress our colorful, creative, or "odd" aspects. When we grow up, if we've abandoned our unique characteristics, we may feel lost, frustrated, and meaningless. Embracing your uniqueness in how you dress, act, and present your inspired insights, you can change the world for the better. Look at the impacts made by Elton John in music, Hunter Thompson in journalism, and Georgia O'Keefe in art. As the Smash Mouth song, All–Star goes, "Only shooting stars break the mold."

About Gail: Gail Rubin is a Certified Thanatologist, a pioneering death educator who uses humor, funny film clips, and outside–the–box activities to get people to plan ahead for our 100% mortality rate. She introduced the worldwide Death Café movement to the United States in 2012, and she created one–day Before I Die Festivals in 2019.

Known as The Doyenne of Death®, she's an award–winning professional speaker who "knocked 'em dead" with her TEDx talk, "A Good Goodbye." She has authored three books on end–of–life issues: A GOOD GOODBYE: Funeral Planning for Those Who Don't Plan to Die, HAIL AND FAREWELL: Cremation Ceremonies, Templates and Tips, and KICKING THE BUCKET LIST: 100 Downsizing and Organizing Things to Do Before You Die.

She's an informed advocate for planning ahead, a Certified Funeral Celebrant, and a respected voice in the funeral industry. She also created The Newly–Dead Game®, a fun way for couples and individuals to focus on planning ahead for end–of–life issues. Albuquerque Business First recognized her with their 2019 Women of Influence award.

64

ALWAYS BE ON THE LOOKOUT FOR OPPORTUNITIES TO SEIZE - DARLENE T. CARVER

The Habit: Always be on the lookout for opportunities to seize

By Darlene T. Carver – Educational Entrepreneur

Why: When something happens that looks like it could be a good direction for you, a challenging option, a chance to do something you have not done before, a new skill to add to your toolbox or any other opportunity – TAKE IT. We say that "someday I will do..." and then other things happen that become obstacles and prevent us from realizing what we want. Find the time to plan your dreams and seize the opportunity.

ABOUT DARLENE: Darlene T. Carver had a dream to own her own business school and seized the opportunity when she was only 25 years old. She researched the location, networked within the community, developed a marketing plan, and with minimal investment, signed a lease, bought furniture and equipment, wrote curricula, set up office procedures, developed marketing materials, and began the process of ascertaining approval from the Maryland State Board of Higher Education to operate as a school called Abbie Business Institute (ABI). Within four years, ABI received national accreditation. The school continued to grow, and by the time Darlene sold the school ten years later, ABI had moved three times to larger facilities, doubling the space each time. Almost 40 years later, the business is still in existence. Because Darlene was always passionate about training, she started a training company, Merlin & Associates, Inc., and works with corporations and government agencies providing essential skills training to help improve productivity. Darlene has been recognized by the U.S. Small Business Administration as a Small Business Training Advocate two years in a row. The Governor of Maryland gave her a Citation for "commitment to the people of Maryland...by making a difference in their lives and employment experiences."

RAISING THE BAR-SETTING HIGHER EXPECTATIONS AND EXCEEDING THEM - BRANDON B. KELLY

The Habit: Raising the Bar–Setting Higher Expectations and exceeding them

By Brandon B. Kelly PhD, CPM – Founder of CEO Super Summit; Founder of National Association of CEO's, International Speaker & Author

Why: Most people are guilty of either not setting goals and aspirations, or not setting them high enough to truly grow from that expectation. After facing life–threatening cancer, I have tried to raise the bar in all I do with each day and goal that I have, and it has placed me in with the stars! Look for the high bar or mark of distinction, and then shoot to have a higher or better outcome. Look at the records that can be beaten, then set that as the target. Expect to reach a higher milestone, and you will. Expect mediocrity, and you will stay mediocre. Expect nothing, and you will accomplish nothing. Those high achievers have made it a habit to keep improving, keep raising the bar, and they expect to be a star simply because they have elevated their efforts to elevate their excellence. This habit will help you in raising your expectations, your goals, your income, and your performance.

ABOUT BRANDON: Brandon Kelly is the author of 5 books, started and sold nine businesses, set 3 high jump records, competed for a spot on the US Olympic High Jump team, part of two Guinness Book of World Records, and was presented an award from the King of Sweden for serving youth around the world. He is the founder of the International CEO Super Summit and The National Society of CEOs. Brandon has also written or contributed more than 150 national courses and training on leadership and goal setting. He also serves on 4 National Committees and Boards of Directors.

He married his teenage sweetheart, and together they have 4 children and recently celebrated their 22nd anniversary. Brandon Kelly is the author of 5 books, started and sold 9 businesses, set 3 high jump records, competed for a spot on the US Olympic High Jump team, part of two Guinness Book of World Records, and was presented an award from the King of Sweden for serving youth around the world. He is the founder of the

International CEO Super Summit and The National Society of CEOs. Brandon has also written or contributed more than 150 national courses and trainings on leadership and goal setting. He also serves on 4 National Committees and Boards of Directors. He married his teenage, and together they have 4 children and recently celebrated their 22nd anniversary.

LISTEN TO WHAT'S BEING SAID (AND WHAT'S NOT BEING SAID) - MIKE TANKEL

The Habit: Listen to what's being said (and what's not being said)

By Mike Tankel – Partner/Optimist, To Be Continued

Why: People sometimes ask, why are you so quiet? It's not that I am quiet, it's that I am listening so that the words I use have meaning and impact. I believe that listening is the ultimate sign of respect—when we listen, we learn, we appreciate, we let the speaking party know they matter. But more than that, we absorb, we take in the information, process it and are then able to converse and accept or challenge with passion, with emotion, and with care. It keeps us from jumping to conclusions while offering valued counsel. And, I know for me, it makes my words more meaningful as I have paid attention, showed I care and can respond both intelligently and respectfully. Even when I am wrong.

 **ABOUT MIKE:** Mike Tankel is an industry leading marketing and strategic executive having served the brand, agency and entertainment worlds for over 25 years, unearthing creative insights, delivering emotional messaging and maximizing story for impact from households to board rooms, start–ups to Fortune 100, domestic to international. Mike's range of experience has seen him as a Fortune 10 brand marketer, growing advertising agencies, and combining strategic marketing with Hollywood magic to contribute to some of the biggest entertainment franchises in history. His un–siloed approach to thinking helps generate quantifiable results, earned media, and long term relationships. He has worked across automotive, telecom, hospitality, technology, entertainment and more, now advising filmmakers, VR practitioners, cannabis brands and bitcoin leaders building global teams, trust, and results.

FOCUS ON SOLUTIONS INSTEAD OF PROBLEMS - TED MA

The Habit: Focus on solutions instead of problems

By Ted Ma – Keynote Speaker and Leadership Expert

Why: You can't control what happens to you, but you can control how you respond. When a problem arises, most people allow the issue to consume their attention. This often leads to unnecessary stress, frustration, and situations getting blown out of proportion. Shifting your focus from the problem to the solution redirects your energy. Instead of getting caught up in negative emotions and wondering, "why is this happening to me?" your attention moves to "what can I do about it?" Focusing on solutions helps you avoid feeling like a victim and forces you to take responsibility for what you can do to improve the outcome.

About Ted: Ted Ma helps organizations develop better leaders and a more engaged workforce. He has been leading teams and developing leaders for over 17 years, having built an international sales team of over 6,000 independent agents. Ted was named one of the top 100 keynote speakers for 2019 by Databird Research Journal and has been featured in numerous publications including Kiplinger, CNBC, Inc, and the New York Times. He is a member of the National Speakers Association and has shared the stage with speakers like Mel Robbins, John Maxwell, and Jack Canfield. His high–energy speaking style combines motivation with education, interaction, and actionable takeaways.

68

CRAFT A POWERFUL AND COMPELLING VISION AND REGULARLY IMAGINE YOURSELF ACHIEVING IT - ABBY DONNELLY

The Habit: Craft a powerful and compelling vision and regularly imagine yourself achieving it

By Abby Donnelly – Founder and CEO of The Leadership & Legacy Group

Why: There is tremendous power in getting clear on who you are and what you want for your life. By putting pen to paper, or fingers to keyboard, you articulate it, document it, refine it and bring it to life. Over time, the words become your experience, and the vision becomes your reality. I've been practicing this habit for over 30 years, and it has transformed my life.

About Abby: Abby is the founder of The Leadership & Legacy Group. She works closely with business owners to

develop their leaders for succession and to help them discover a meaningful and rewarding next chapter. Abby is a 14–year veteran of Procter & Gamble, where she facilitated strategic planning and led category–wide process improvement efforts. She was a partner at a Sandler Training franchise, and she is a graduate of the University of Florida with a Master of Statistics. Abby serves on the board of First Bank of North Carolina (FBNC) and has published several books including Straight Talk About Planning Your Succession: A Primer for CEOs and 128 Tips to Make You a More Effective Leader.

69

BE SO GOOD, THEY CAN'T IGNORE YOU
- AMY LESLIE

The Habit: Be so good, they can't ignore you

By Amy Leslie – CEO of Perspective Consulting

Why: Sometimes, life is just not fair. There will be a time when you get passed up, don't make the team, or don't get what you deserve because someone else is part of the "in–crowd." Favoritism is part of life, and sometimes you are not the favorite. When this happens, you have two choices:

- You can complain about it and give up because "it doesn't matter what I do, I can't win" or
- You can dig in, work harder, and be so good they can't ignore you!

About Amy: Amy Leslie is CEO of Perspective Consulting, a management consulting firm. Amy is passionate about helping other leaders avoid the mistakes she made early in her career. Her firm specializes in assisting companies to use proven, scientifically valid tools, and methodologies to avoid bad hiring decisions, manage people better, and essentially create a more productive and happy workforce. Her company also teaches leaders how to inspire their people to greatness. Amy is also a wife and stepmom.

70

FIND YOUR 100% EFFORT - JONAH WHITE

The Habit: Find your 100% effort

By Jonah White – Entrepreneur, Author and Public Speaker

Why: When you find your 100%, it will become your most potent weapon.

The Millennial mindset is to "work smarter not harder" Most of the growing workforce views hard work as a sign of failure. I am living proof that this is not the case.

Most people only give 40% to 60% effort toward their passions in life. This includes their business.

If you give what everyone else gives you will probably end up in the same place. This means there is a 90%

chance that your new business venture will fail, just like all the other startups.

• Embrace hardship.

• Work long hours.

• Do the work that makes other people cringe.

• Be a generalist who overwhelms the obstacle course.

• When you are not physically working, make sure your mind is always working – 24/7.

• Make sure you are always figuring out problems before they happen.

• Look for new product lines and do things that other people only are will to do during working (daylight) hours.

The Entrepreneur who gives 100% is always on point..always ready with a plan B and even a plan C.

Then when you are comfortable (If that is ever the case) with the growth of your company, then you can back off the throttle and focus on other things.

 **About Jonah:** Jonah White Is a self–made multi–millionaire, Who grew up dirt poor in a log cabin with no running water in rural Illinois. He is one of the founders of Billy–Bob Teeth Inc. He and his partner Rich

Bailey made more than 50 million dollars by actually making people look ugly. Billy Bob teeth are sold in more than 150 countries from around the world, and so far, they have manufactured and sold more than 20 million of them. Jonah is also a Public Speaker and Author. He wrote the book "The Billy Bob Secret to Life" that tells his rags to riches story. Life growing up poor to a successful business owner today.

71

START YOUR DAY WITH ENTHUSIASM - NAOMI BAREKET

The Habit: Start your day with ENTHUSIASM

By Naomi Bareket – Author, Speaker, & Success Coach

Why: Because how you start your day, every day, is how you live your life. And how do you start your day with ENTHUSIASM? As soon as you open your eyes in the morning, say "wow, thank you G–d for giving me a new day, for believing in me, for trusting in me to fulfill my mission." Remember, the word ENTHUSIASM also means with G–d inside. So naturally, this magical habit fuels you with ENTHUSIASM, a push forward inspiration to manifest the best in you. This will boost up your productivity and success, light your spark, and will positively reflect on every person you will socialize with.

 **About Naomi:** Naomi Bareket is a Speaker and dynamic Seminar Leader who uses modern techniques and Kabbalistic wisdom to facilitate you to own your power, take charge of your mind, realize your motivator factors, and be in congruence internally and with your team. Bareket is the co–creator of NeuroSUCCESSology™ whereby she offers her broad experience in linguistics, Time Line Therapy®, hypnosis, neuroscience, Kabbalah, and the field of Neuro–Linguistic Programming (NLP) to empower you to create lives of fulfillment.

She has been certified by John Maxwell as a Leadership Coach, Teacher, Trainer, and Speaker, and she is certified by the American Board of NLP to train and certify others as NLP practitioners and masters. Bareket is also the author of THE DEEP SEE: How to See into your Soul and Find Who You Are and Want to Be. She loves to combine business with spiritual work. Therefore, she loves to work with entrepreneurs, business owners, coaches, and speakers. Naomi believes that when you live in alignment with your true self, you can fulfill your life's purpose and live a meaningful life.

72

MAKE EVERY INTERACTION A POSITIVE ONE - ALVIN LAW

The Habit: Make every interaction a positive one

By Alvin Law – Motivational Speaker & Bestselling Author

Why: E–R–O! Little did I know I have practiced this habit all my life. That famous Co–Author of the Chicken Soup books, Jack Canfield identified in his book "The Success Principles" that "E +/– R = O." "Event (plus) Positive or Negative Response (equals) Outcome!" Every day we face a variety of events in our lives. We have within each of us, the power to choose a positive or negative response to those events, which in turn directly affects the outcome of that event. The "Habit" is about choosing a "Positive" response, which almost always ends in a "Positive" Outcome! It does work...trust me!

ABOUT ALVIN: Alvin Law is one of Canada's first "Thalidomide Babies," infants born with birth defects caused by the infamous morning sickness medication. Alvin was born without arms. He was also given up for adoption at five days of age. But his life path was altered by foster parents who gave Alvin a home, taught him to use his feet for hands but more importantly, never allowed Alvin to blame anyone or make excuses! "There's No Such Word As Can't" was the mantra Alvin embraced. He played trombone in the school band, plays the drums and piano and even drives a car with no adaptive equipment. Today, he's married, a dad, a Bestselling Author and a world-class, Hall of Fame, Canadian Motivational Speaker!

73

MAKE THE TREND YOUR FRIEND - DANIEL LEVINE

The Habit: Make the Trend Your Friend

By Daniel Levine – Trends Experts

Why: Learning to use all your senses – not just to understand where you are, but to see where you are going – is a key to success when making up your mind. This is an excellent tool in business, health, love, and life. If things are not moving in the direction you would like them to, noticing this trend early is the advance notice you need to jump in fast and make a positive change. On the other hand, if you perceive that things are going your way, relish the fact that you can just sit back and let good things happen all by themselves.

ABOUT DANIEL: Daniel Levine is one of the world's best–known trends experts. Hailed as a "genius" by Elle magazine and "the ultimate guru of cool" by CNN, he is the author of over 20 Bestselling books and a frequent guest on international television. As the Director of a New York–based trends consultancy, Daniel is the leader of a large international team of trend–spotters who track the latest ideas and experiences from around the globe. From Intel and Pfizer to BMW and American Express, Daniel helps top businesses embrace trends to be more relevant, innovative, and profitable.

74

BELIEVE THAT EVERYONE IS DOING THE BEST THEY KNOW HOW - KATIE MARES

The Habit: Believe that everyone is doing the best they know how

By Katie Mares – Brand Experience Expert

Why: I grew up in a family of alcohol abuse and addiction. I raised my sister and brother, and my parents were not around; life was anything but easy. Today I have a relationship with both of my parents and can say that I am grateful that I do. I often get asked, how did you get through life, remain positive, have success, and develop a relationship with your parents? My answer is this; I believe that everyone is doing the best that they can with the tools they are given. How can we expect more from someone that may not know any better? Having this frame of mind allows you to meet every person where they stand and build relationships from that starting point. It will enable you to enter into every situation with a positive frame of mind and belief that each person is doing their best with the tools they have. When you believe this, you become more patient, understanding, and compassionate towards others and their story.

ABOUT KATIE: Katie knows first hand the challenges organizations and their encounter as they strive to design a customer service program that is sustainable and has an impact in the marketplace. She also knows that developing a program is just one small step to success, it is the tools and implementation plan that makes a program take flight.

Using her experiences as a Chief Inspiration Officer, building company infrastructure and designing customer experience programs, Katie is now a leading voice inspiring positive, actionable change in the organizations she partners with. Katie has earned her Master's in Adult Training and Development and is a Certified Training & Development Professional.

As a Certified Speaking Professional, Katie has inspired audiences around the world to think differently about customer service and leadership. She imparts skills to change behavior, which has a positive effect on the experience offered to customers and team members.

Katie has a unique approach; she focuses on developing the C.O.R.E. confidence and skills of team members when creating tailored standards for each organization and its customer. Katie has worked with globally recognized brands such as Honda, Celebrity Cruises, and Canada Post. Her delivery is concise, emotional, and impactful! Audiences who experience Katie, walk away inspired to make positive, actionable changes and are ready to use their new skills to change the experience your brand provides their customers and team members.

Katie lives in Toronto with her husband and their three children. When she is not traveling around the world consulting and speaking, Katie can be found on a yoga mat (in a shoe store!) or snuggled on the couch with her three little ones eating homemade popcorn and watching a movie!

75

2X THE DAY - DAVE SWANSON

The Habit: 2X the day

By Dave Swanson – Keynote Speaker and Leadership Trainer

Why: You can't double your day production. Understood. 2X the day means do 2 things that go towards your next dream or goal at least twice a day, no matter how big or how small it is. Because it is progress and before you know it, in the next year you will have had over 700 actions towards making your dream or goal come true. Put it somewhere where you see it every day and take the time to send that text, send that email or do some research as long as you are making positive progress.

ABOUT DAVE: Dave had less than a 1% chance of getting into West Point, so he went and did it anyway. Dave Swanson is a combat Veteran who experienced over 100 firefights during his tour of duty. He was a Platoon Leader during the infamous 'Black Sunday' in Sadr City, Iraq in 2004, an event that is now highlighted in the series, "The Long Road Home" on National Geographic. He is the author of two books, "The Dot on the Left" and "Resilient Leadership."

Swanson aims to identify and activate the hidden potential in individuals and processes. Through all of his endeavors, he motivates and empowers change in others. Dave also reaches high school and college students to help change the attitude and path of those labeled as 'under–performers.' Dave is passionate about educating and advancing our nation's youth and has become known as a "Millennial Whisperer" due to the success of his leadership training for millennials. Dave's LAWs have enabled him to bicycle across America, summit Mt. Rainier, and receive the Leadership and Service Award from the University of Texas' McCombs School of Business. He is currently pursuing his Ph.D. in Leadership.

76

KEEP AN EYE ON YOUR REPUTATION - ROY SMOOTHE

The Habit: Keep An Eye on Your Reputation

By Roy Smoothe – #1 Amazon / ITunes Author, Publisher, Speaker, and Branding Consultant

Why: Your Reputation Arrives Before You Do & Remains After You've Left.

I have always believed you should 'Be the best you, and do your best for others'

In life and business, you'll find that a lot of success is based on who knows what you are like, more than who knows what you do or know. People are happy to start and develop long term relationships with people who have a good reputation.

A bad reputation is tough to clear up. Once someone

thinks badly of you, they'll remember that, even when it's time to find someone to do whatever you're capable of doing.

One of the most exciting parts of being a young person is all the potential you hold. You have the power and ability to be anything you want to be if you will be the person others want to be with.

All the dreams are within your reach if you have an excellent reputation.

About Roy: Known as the Cool Branding Guy, Roy Smoothe is an #1 Amazon / Itunes Author, Publisher, Speaker, and Branding Consultant.

Roy is the founder of the Cool People Group and CEO of Smoothe Media, a cutting edge audio production and publishing company which leverage's leading–edge technologies to drive personal development and business performance improvements.

Roy creates world–class projects and high–impact initiatives that improve the way people live, learn, work, and do business. He believes fashion, music, and personal development are always changing and morphing into something that you can apply to individual and company branding.

As a speaker and presenter Roy's speeches, workshops,

seminars, and the Smoothe Mixx motivational messaging have been used effectively in programs for business and enterprise, personal development, self–esteem, developing confidence, and also enhancing elite sports performance.

77

DAILY PHYSICAL EXERCISE - DOUG GRADY

The Habit: Daily physical exercise

By Doug Grady – Author and Speaker

Why: When I was a young boy, I was shy, quiet, introverted, and self–conscious. Physical exercise, first known as "play" (in the backyard, on swingsets, climbing trees...) always gave me a sense of joy and freedom. In eighth grade, I participated in organized sports for the first time as a wrestler. Practices were rigorous and demanding. This developed a sense of confidence and leadership I had previously not expressed. As a man, physical exercise continues to be the single most important habit in my life. It helps to create conditions favorable for an experience of peace, connection, and power. Every area of my life is positively affected when I am consistently engaged in physical disciplines. It also supports the development of other healthy habits, many of which you will read about in this book.

 ABOUT DOUG: Doug Grady has been studying and teaching the pathways to personal potential for over 20 years. Doug is a highly requested keynote speaker and is the author of The Ripple Effect. He also developed the life–changing program 40 Days of FOCUS.

Doug gives a significant portion of his time and money to local and global causes. He has been on several mission trips, most recently to Ecuador where he was part of a twelve man team building homes for the poorest of the poor.

His companies, writings, training, and music are designed with one purpose: to help people reach their God–given potential.

78

BE CONFIDENT IN WHERE YOU STAND - MICHELLE LEE SKALETSKI-BOYD

The Habit: Be Confident in Where You Stand

By Michelle lee Skaletski–Boyd – Intuitive Medium & Bestselling Author

Why: When someone questions your character, it is human to question your position. Instead, pause for a moment to reflect then ask your self, "is this my truth?" Should you know in your heart their perception is off, rather than take a defensive position that moves you out of alignment and keeps you stuck in resistance and the need to be right, stay aligned with your higher self, send thanks for your stronger sense of knowing, and continue to walk the higher road.

ABOUT MICHELLE LEE: Michelle lee Skaletski–Boyd, The Corporate Woo–Woo™ is both business–minded and a little bit 'out there.' After graduating with honors, she climbed the corporate ladder. Making her way through a career path, she worked for both traditional and online advertising agencies as well a Fortune 500 and the nation's largest privately–held telecommunications company where she led and managed key accounts.

In 2006, Michelle lee moved to Montana with her husband Steven and traded in her high heels for hiking boots. After forming her business to help others with soul discoveries, Michelle lee earned the title of "Best Psychic Medium" for nearly four years and then amicably parted ways from this position so she could focus more on a writing career. Her sequel of books "Words for the Soul: Heaven–Sent Life Lessons and Conversations with God" became #1 best–sellers overnight.

Today Michelle lee is a long–standing member of the International Medical and Dental Hypnotherapy Association, a Reiki Master Teacher, Clinically Certified Hypnotherapist and Intuitive Medium. She has taken thousands of people around the globe on powerful soul journeys both in–person and on retreat. By being in Michelle lee's presence, you are invited to become more aware of your own.

79

BE THE PRESIDENT OF YOUR OWN FAN CLUB - TRACY LITT

The Habit: Be the President of Your Own Fan Club

By Tracy Litt – Certified Mindset Coach, RTT and Author

Why: Nothing is more important than the words you say to yourself. Developing and maintaining empowering self–talk builds unstoppable confidence and iron–clad belief. From there, everything you desire is possible.

Every word you say is a directive that your mind, body, and psyche work to make real. So being mindful of how you speak to yourself and choosing the language that is loving, kind, encouraging, and supportive will enable you to reach your highest levels of success while experiencing joy and fulfillment. Being the President of Your Own Fan Club also means cultivating self–compassion and meeting yourself with love and understanding even when something doesn't go the way you intended. The relationship you have with yourself is the most important relationship in your life. Practicing empowering and loving self–talk is key to nurturing that relationship.

 **ABOUT TRACY:** If Brene Brown and Tony Robbins had a baby, that baby would be Tracy. She's direct and goes straight to the heart of what's real and what's true. She masterfully tells it like it is while being skillfully empathetic, loving, and supportive. A powerhouse and ball of energy, exuding unconditional love and light. Silly and playful. She calls your bullshit and wakes you up in a way you never realized you needed. Tracy Litt is a Certified Mindset Coach, Rapid Transformational Therapist, Speaker, and Author of Worthy Human. She is the founder of The Litt Factor, a personal growth and coaching company.

Tracy exists to remind you of your potential, teach you the power of your mind, and support you in cultivating a phenomenal relationship with yourself. It is through this unwavering belief in yourself, tremendous self–love and inner strength that you can feel, create, and be anything and everything you desire.

80

HELP EVERYONE YOU POSSIBLY CAN WITH ABSOLUTELY NO EXPECTATION OF RECEIVING ANYTHING IN RETURN - GREG VETTER

The Habit: Help everyone you possibly can with absolutely no expectation of receiving anything in return

By Greg Vetter – Corporate Trainer, Speaker and Author

Why: My brother John and I grew up in a small town called Riverhead on eastern Long Island during the 1950s. Dad owned a construction business and continuously worked to maintain it. We were lucky to get away as a family for a brief vacation, and we almost always drove.

One summer, my family returned from a trip to Connecticut across Long Island Sound. We had just left the ferry and were headed back to Riverhead when my father suddenly pulled the car over. Another vehicle was parked off on the side of the road. A woman, looking slightly bewildered, stood beside the car, and stared at it as though something was wrong. As Dad stepped out of our car, he assured us that he would return shortly.

When Dad slipped back into our trusty Ford, he swung his arm over the seat to get a good look at John and me. He said, "Boys, always remember to help everyone you possibly can with absolutely no expectation of receiving anything in return. You help someone because you can."

With that, John and I learned one of life's greatest lessons: The joy of pure giving and expecting nothing in return.

This is still one of the most vivid memories I have of my childhood.

Thanks, Dad.

ABOUT GREG: Greg Vetter is President of Vetter Productivity Inc., an organizational training firm founded in Atlanta in 1989 and author of the books Find It In 5 Seconds and Winning The Productivity Game. Greg creates work processes and systems that enable you to work smarter, faster, and more efficiently—that is, produce more in less time and with less stress.

Greg teaches his organizational system, A Vetter Way®

consisting of a system of how to work, a system of how to find information in 5 seconds that can be used with any technology or paper system, and a system of how to identify and continually work on your one key activity.

Greg has helped hundreds of companies across the country, including personally coaching and organizing one-on-one, with over 150 officers and employees of The Coca-Cola Company®.

81

DON'T SEND IMPORTANT COMMUNICATIONS WITHOUT WAITING AT LEAST ONE NIGHT - BUCK JONES

THE HABIT: Don't send important communications without waiting at least one night

By Buck Jones – Corporate Trainer and Educator

Why: No matter how good I think the piece is, (and yes, I write some great pieces at 10:00 PM, ... don't we all?), I find the next morning, after rereading and making a few changes, my new piece will be much more reflective of me, and the message I genuinely want to convey.

By waiting until the next day, I can remove any unnecessary emotion (Do you ever get too emotional?), and my word choice, punctuation and grammar will be much better. In short, I can convey the message I want to send, at a much higher level, ... and isn't that what we are honestly trying to accomplish anyway?

So try it. Write the best piece you can. Make it extraordinary, ... make it earth–shattering, ... change the world, ... then, when you finally get it finished, ... no matter how excited you are, ... hold yourself back, ... and push the 'Save' button, not the 'Send' button. Get a good night's sleep, and then reread your piece the next morning. You will be amazed at how specific changes, changes you never saw the night before, will jump right out at you.

This simple habit will, ... save you much grief, ... allow you to communicate at a higher level, ... present you and your ideas on a new plane.

About Buck: Buck Jones is an experienced leader and international consultant with expertise in retail and manufacturing. He spent over 25 years as a retailer, starting as a part–timer while in high school, and ending up as a corporate Vice President for one of the largest grocery companies in the U.S. He formed his own company in the early '90s and has been working with manufacturers and retailers in the U.S., Brazil, and Europe ever since.

As an acclaimed trainer and educator, he developed and managed a retail training program used by more than

16,000 supermarkets for over ten years, ... as a speaker, he is a member of the National Speakers Association and has been featured on almost every retail platform in the country, ... moreover, as an author, he wrote his industry magazine column for six years, wrote and starred in more than four dozen videos, and has written two books. He is an educator, thinker, speaker, and coach.

82

ELIMINATE THE NEGATIVES - VAN C. DEEB

The Habit: Eliminate the negatives

By Van C. Deeb – Author, Entrepreneur, Motivational and Inspirational Speaker

Why: When I was building my company, first and foremost, I would always find ways to stay positive and eliminate the negative influences in my life. You know the old saying "Misery loves company" It is crucial for you to remember that you are the average of the 5 people you choose to be around the most. Being cynical, complaining, critical and judgmental is contagious, so make sure you limit your exposure around these types of people. Think about how good you feel when you are around someone that has a positive attitude and a smile on their face. I avoided negative influences at all costs and still do that same practice today. Watch what happens to your life when you eliminate the negatives out of yours. Make this your habit!

ABOUT VAN: Van Deeb is a native of Omaha, Nebraska. After playing football at the University of Nebraska Omaha, he attended a real estate specialty school in Dallas, Texas. Van sold real estate in Dallas for 10 years before moving back home to Omaha to open up DEEB Realty in 1993.

Van started his company with just himself out of his basement and grew it to one of the largest Real Estate firms in the Midwest with over 350 agents in only 15 years. Van sold DEEB Realty in January of 2009 and now travels the country inspiring and motivating Salespeople and Business owners to be the best they can be.

83

READ GREAT NOVELS/LITERATURE - CRAIG TITLEY

The Habit: Read great novels/literature

By Craig Titley – Feature Film and TV Writer/Producer

Why: If you're reading this, then I'm going to guess... you like to read. Or at least you will tolerate reading to be informed or to learn and grow. Almost every high achiever I know reads quite a bit, but few of them read anything other than non-fiction, business, or self-improvement books (also all worthwhile but...). They fall into the trap of thinking fiction is, at worst, a non-productive waste of time or, at best, a frivolous entertainment. They are wrong.

Whether it's the classics (Moby Dick, The Great Gatsby, Huckleberry Finn, Pride and Prejudice, the plays of

William Shakespeare) or modern fiction and Nobel Prize-winning novels, make it a habit to read a bit every day.

Why fiction? Because the really great works will stir your soul in ways that non-fiction will not. These novels are created by great minds using fiction as a means to explore the human condition, to try to touch upon the universal by writing about specific events or characters. Reading great literature will shake up and challenge the way you see and understand the world by forcing you to walk in someone else's shoes... to live in their head. And as a bonus... you quite often get to time travel to the past in which the stories are set. So pick one up (there are plenty of "100 Greatest Novels Ever Written" lists out there to get you started) and read.

And, yes, I said read. Listening (to books on tape), does not count. Sure, there has been a lot of reliable science confirming there's no noticeable difference in retention from actually reading the word on the page to listening to the words being read, but... grow up! Do the work yourself. You don't need mommy or daddy or the celebrity voice du jour to read to you! The unplugging is part of the habit and part of the joy. Get your nose down in those pages and breathe it in. It's the greatest most transformative smell in the world.

Personally, I read for one hour every morning with my breakfast, and one hour every night before I go to bed. On weekends, I'll usually try to set aside a nice big block of time (usually on a Sunday afternoon) to read. Quite often, cigars are involved. At that rate, I can usually finish a novel every 1-2 weeks. I also make it a habit of taking the book I'm reading everywhere I go. A little extra time before a meeting: I read. Waiting for a doctor's appointment: I read. The beauty of this habit is: you can do it anywhere. At a beachside café, under a tree in a park, at your favorite diner... Whether you want to commit to a certain amount of reading per day (one hour, ten pages) or simply set a goal of completing three great novels every year, it's your call to make... and once you make it, it's your call to adventure and enlightenment. So get going!

 **About Craig:** Craig Titley is a feature film and television writer/producer who began his film career in the Hollywood trenches as a production assistant for feature films and television movies. He spent three years in film development as an assistant story editor for director Joe Dante (Gremlins, Innerspace) and a creative executive for Nickelodeon Movies before going on to become a successful screenwriter, penning the first live-action Scooby-Doo movie (co-story with James Gunn), Cheaper by the Dozen (story), and Percy Jackson & The Olympians: The Lightning Thief. His latest feature film projects include adaptations of Twenty Thousand Leagues Under the Sea (with Sam Raimi producing), Arabian Nights, and Dean Koontz's Oddkins. Titley's films have grossed nearly a billion dollars in worldwide box office.

In television, Titley worked with George Lucas and

Lucasfilm Animation, penning episodes of Star Wars: The Clone Wars. He was a writer/producer on the NBC super-hero series The Cape and is an Executive Producer and Writer on Marvel's Agents of S.H.I.E.L.D.

Titley was born in Mattoon, Illinois. He is a graduate of Eastern Illinois University (with degrees in both English and Business Management), received his MFA from the University of Southern California's Peter Stark Program, and is completing a Ph.D. in Mythological Studies at Pacifica Grrduate Institute, home of the Joseph Campbell library. He recently launched Discount Anarchy, an all-in entertainment company for film and television production, publishing, games, music, artist management and concert promotion.

84

CREATE A DAILY HABIT MACHINE - DAVID MELTZER

The Habit: Create a daily habit machine

By David Meltzer – Keynote Speaker, Author, Business Coach and Entrepreneur

W hy: The most impactful habit you can have is a system of creating positive habits. When you understand how specific cues trigger an action, and how the feedback or reward from that behavior causes it to become a repetitive action, you can then substitute positive habits for negative ones quickly and easily using a combination of skills, knowledge, and desire. Creating a system that helps you to build positive routines will always lead to more productivity and accessibility, no matter where you are in life.

ABOUT DAVID: David Meltzer is the CEO of Sports 1 Marketing, one of the world's leading sports & entertainment marketing agencies, which he co–founded with Hall of Fame Quarterback Warren Moon. David previously served as the CEO of Samsung's first smartphone division, CEO of the famous Leigh Steinberg Sports and Entertainment Agency (the inspiration for the movie Jerry Maguire), and is currently the Chairman of the Unstoppable Foundation, a non–profit humanitarian organization bringing sustainable education to children and communities in developing countries. He is also a renowned keynote speaker, author, business coach, and entrepreneur, who was named Sports Humanitarian of the Year by Variety and has been named a top speaker to hire by outlets such as Forbes and Entrepreneur. He has written two Bestselling books, Connected to Goodness and Be Unstoppable, and his newest book from McGraw–Hill, Game–Time Decision Making, features a foreword from Tilman Fertitta, CEO of Landry's, Inc., and owner of the NBA's Houston Rockets. David has also been recognized as one of the world's best business advisors, being named by renowned executive coach Marshall Goldsmith as one of his Top 100 Business Coaches.

85

WRITE SOMETHING EVERY DAY - SHAWN EDWARDS

The Habit: Write something every day

By Shawn Edwards – Co–Founder – African American Film Critics Association

Why: First of all, this is not just a habit for a writer. This is a habit for everyone. The more you write, the better you get at writing, and the more creative you become in life in general. It's that simple. The art of writing starts with you just doing it. Don't worry about how perfect it is. Just get your thoughts out. However, the process gets much easier if you do it regularly. And it doesn't matter how you do it — on a laptop, on paper, on the phone or on a napkin. Just write. It can be for something formal, a journal for yourself, or just to entertain yourself. The critical thing is craft sentences and construct paragraphs. The next thing you know words will pour out of you like Niagara Falls. Don't be afraid of writer's block or creative lapses. This is not a cure for that. Just simply write. This simple exercise opens up creativity in your life that will flow to all other walks of your life.

ABOUT SHAWN: Shawn Edwards is a journalist, TV and film producer and marketing and event consultant. As a nationally recognized film critic for Fox 4 News in Kansas City, Missouri he has won numerous national awards including Best TV Film Critic twice by the LA Press Club's National Entertainment Journalism Awards. Edwards has produced numerous TV shows and documentaries. Edwards co–founded the African American Film Critics Association in 2003 and has produced its award show that takes place annually in LA. Edwards also created 'A Celebration of Black Cinema' in conjunction with the Broadcast Film Critics Association which premiered in 2014 in Los Angeles at the House of Blues Sunset. Edwards created iloveblackmovies in 2008, the popular website, web series and clothing line. He currently works at Hidden Empire Film Group, based in Los Angeles, as a Creative Marketing Specialist. He is a life–long lover of movies who began making his own films in the 7th grade.

86

MEDITATE EVERY DAY - TOM CRONIN

The Habit: Meditate Every Day

By Tom Cronin – Producer and Co–Writer of The Portal
Film and Book

Why: When I introduced daily meditation into my life, I experienced a significant turning point that helped reduced chronic stress, and helped me live a healthier and happier life. Since that day 23 years ago, I have made meditation a part of my day, every day. It is a technique that not only keeps my body optimized and healthy but improves my brain functionality, reduces cortisol, and increases serotonin and oxytocin. Having taught thousands of people all over the world, I feel the best advice I can give to someone is to continue to sit in the stillness and calm the mind through meditation daily.

 **ABOUT TOM:** Tom Cronin spent 26 years in financial markets as one of Sydney's leading bond and swap brokers. He discovered meditation in the early stages of his career, when the anxiety and chaos he was experiencing had hit a crisis point, and it completely transformed his world, both personally and professionally. Founder of The Stillness Project, a global movement to inspire one billion people to sit in stillness daily, Tom is passionate about reducing stress and chaos in people's lives. His ongoing work in transformational leadership and cultivating inner peace through meditation takes him around the world hosting retreats, mentoring, presenting keynote talks, teaching and creating The Portal film–book experience, all part of his commitment to the current planetary shift.

87

HANDSOME IS AS HANDSOME DOES - JAMES WHITTAKER

The Habit: Handsome is as handsome does

By James Whittaker – Author / co–executive producer of
Think and Grow Rich: The Legacy

Why: My Dad used to say this to us over and over again when we were kids. Many years later, I still continue to appreciate the powerful and concise meaning behind it. It doesn't matter what we wish for, what background we come from, or what outfit we wear, it is our actions—and actions alone—that are the real determinant of character. The best part? One simple act, available to all of us, can illuminate the world one person at a time.

About James: James Whittaker was born in Australia and currently resides in Los Angeles, California, with his wife

 Jenn and their daughter Sophie. After a successful career in financial planning, where he ran a company with more than $2 billion under management,

James has been featured extensively in television, print and digital media around the world, including The Today Show, Success Magazine, and The Sydney Morning Herald.

James also appeared on 300+ podcasts and radio shows and spoken to audiences of 2,000+ people. In 2018, he authored Think and Grow Rich: The Legacy as the official companion to the multi–million–dollar film based on Napoleon Hill's timeless classic. James is also a proud co–executive producer of the film. Today, through his various books, speaking, and education projects, he shares the lessons of high performers to help people all over the world take ownership of their financial, physical, and mental health.

88

ADD VALUE TO SOMEONE'S LIFE EVERY DAY - SHARON LECHTER

The Habit: Add value to someone's life every day

By Sharon Lechter – New York Times Bestselling Author, Speaker, Mentor

Why: Success comes from serving a need or solving a problem by giving your time and/or your talents to improve the lives of others. My father would ask me each night, "Have you added value to someone's life today?" A foundation of service creates your legacy each and every day, allowing you to live your legacy. To create maximum impact in this world and inspire others to do the same... add value to one person's life every day.

About Sharon: Sharon Lechter is an entrepreneur, author, philanthropist, international speaker, licensed CPA and Chartered Global Management Accountant. She is the founder and CEO of Pay Your Family First, a financial and entrepreneurial education organization. Sharon is the co–author of the international and New York Times bestseller *Rich Dad Poor Dad* and 14 other books in the Rich Dad series.

Over 10 years as co–Founder and CEO, she led the Rich Dad Company and brand to global success. In 2008, she was asked by the Napoleon Hill Foundation to help re–energize the teachings of Napoleon Hill and has three bestselling books in cooperation with the Foundation, including *Three Feet from Gold, Outwitting the Devil,* Think and Grow Rich for Women. Sharon's next bestseller, SUCCESS and Something Greater will be released in September of 2019.

She is also featured in the 2017 movie *Think and Grow Rich: The Legacy*. Regarded as a global expert on financial literacy, in 2008 she was appointed to the first President's Advisory Council on Financial Literacy and served President Bush and President Obama.

In 2009, Sharon was appointed to the National CPA Financial Literacy Commission as a national spokesperson and was reappointed in 2014. Sharon is a Junior Achievement University of Success Founding

Chancellor and served as Arizona Chairman for the 2020 Women on Boards initiative. Sharon is also a member of the national board for Childhelp, a national organization founded to prevent and treat child abuse.

89

ASK WITHOUT FEAR - JENNIFER AND STEPHANIE SUTTO

The Habit: Ask without fear

By Jennifer and Stephanie Sutto – CEOs of The Glitter Twins

Why: When you ask for what you want without fear of being rejected, opportunities will start opening up for you! When you get into the habit of asking without fear, changes will begin to happen. You'd be surprised to know how much you're missing out on by not asking. Tip: When we get scared about asking for something, we take a deep breath and say 1...2....3...GO! As soon as you say "GO," ask whatever it is you need to ask!

About Jennifer & Stephanie: We asked without fear when we went from being servers in a restaurant to being

 personally mentored by multimillionaire John Shin. As servers in a restaurant, our side hustle was making and selling glitter gels online to people that go to EDM festivals! We sold tens of thousands of dollars worth of glitter gels from Instagram alone, and we never ran a single ad. We wanted to be more serious with our business, so we started going to entrepreneur events! We went to the first Think and Grow Rich event in California! John Shin was doing a whole world tour of events, and this was the first one! We wanted to be on the social media team running the IG stories because that's what we're good at and we know that's how he could reach the millennial audience! So we DM'd him, set up a call, told him our plan on how we can help, and he said no! We didn't let that stop us, though. We bought a one–way flight, the most expensive $2,000 VIP ticket, and we showed up the event and started working it anyway. Then we asked him again, and he said yes! Now, not only are we running the IG stories for his events, but we're sharing our story and speaking at them! Ask without fear, you'll go further than you think!

90

LEARN TO LOVE WHO YOU ARE - CORT DAVIES

The Habit: Learn to love who you are

By Cort Davies – Future Cancer Survivor, Speaker, Producer and Writer

Why: Don't live your life comparing yourself to others and living according to their dreams and values. Live your life following your own dreams and values. Continually remind yourself that you're special and unique. This is truly the greatest gift you can give to yourself. It is the moment where you go from paddling upstream against the current to paddling downstream toward whatever you define as "success."

Also, When you learn to love who you are, your life opens up to infinite possibilities, and your innate creativity comes out and shines as bright as the sun. As Paulo Coelho summarizes in the book The Alchemist, when you are on a journey to fulfill your personal legend, the whole universe conspires to help you achieve it.

ABOUT CORT: In 2017 Cort Davies was diagnosed with one of the rarest forms of cancer on earth called a malignant paraganglioma. He was given just three years to live. Instead of folding under the intense stress of having a late stage cancer, Cort set out on a mission to save his own life. After 7 surgeries, half of his bladder removed, and almost being paralyzed, Cort realized the cancer and his journey were a gift and that his mindset and his resolve to survive was a necessary trait every cancer patient needed to have.

He decided to translate this gift into a docu–series called Cancer Consciousness to help educate cancer patients around the world how to develop a healing mindset, and how to eliminate destructive habits, giving them a better chance at living a longer happier life. His goal is to help initiate healing for thousands of cancer patients worldwide.

91

GIVING BACK - JESSICA RADETSKY

Habit: Giving back

By Jessica Radetsky – Founder of Broadway Hearts

Why: Giving, especially your time, is a wonderful lesson in respect, gratitude, compassion, and how to adapt to unfamiliar circumstances. A mindset of giving can create a positive ripple effect in your own life. Not only are you helping others, and often building community, but I feel giving back has the potential to change the world in a very real and accessible way.

About Jessica: Jessica Radetsky is the founder of Broadway Hearts, a children's hospital outreach group and arts scholarship program. Originally from Santa Cruz, CA, Jessica began studying classical ballet at the

age of five and started dancing professionally at the age of 17. She has performed with The Kirov Opera Ballet, The San Francisco and Los Angeles Opera Ballets, among others. In love with eras past, she also performs with the Jazz Age dance group The Canarsie Wobblers.

In 2009, after losing her beloved father to BRCA–related pancreatic cancer, Jessica became active in genetic cancer outreach and advocacy. Raising awareness for BRCA–related cancer prevention and quality of life issues around the country, she found a real passion for outreach.

In 2017, Jessica founded Broadway Hearts. Inspired by experiences with Make–A–Wish recipients, she focused on the idea of bringing Broadway performers to kids in children's hospitals, who might not be able to make it to the theater. Expanding on the mission, she started an arts scholarship program for these same children. Broadway Hearts is dedicated to her father, Peter Radetsky.

Jessica currently performs on Broadway in The Phantom of the Opera.

92

GET QUIET EVERYDAY - JOE SWEENEY

The Habit: Get quiet everyday

By Joe Sweeney – *New York Times* Bestselling Author

Why: Even if it is just for 5, 10, or 20 minutes each day, when you get quiet, all sorts of messages start to brew up inside of you. As you do this more and more, the results will become palpable. Being quiet in today's crazy busy world will give you the clarity to move forward with your goals and life. Being quiet results in the freedom to eliminate excuses and start to get clear, get free, and get going down your path. This will help you to find the inspiration you need to move forward towards success and happiness. Your success path will literally become illuminated with inspiration and knowledge when you take the time to listen, ponder, and think.

This simple habit can be a game changer if you just do it every day.

ABOUT JOE: Joe Sweeney has spent more than 30 years blending his love of business and passion for sports. He has owned, operated, and sold four manufacturing companies, headed up the Wisconsin Sports Authority, and launched a sports marketing firm.

Joe purchased an equity interest in an investment banking firm and served as president and managing director. He is now an accomplished author, internationally-known speaker and coach, and investor in private equity companies.

Joe's passion is studying human behavior. He has used the fields of sports, business, and military as his laboratory to better understand why certain people outperform others. He is primarily devoted to helping and mentoring young athletes and executives to develop all aspects of their career, business, and life.

Joe has served on 28 boards of directors and is currently active on Wintrust Financial Corporation (WTFC), a publicly traded financial institution. Joe received his BA in Industrial Psychology from Saint Mary's University of Minnesota and his MBA from the University of Notre Dame.

Joe is the author of three books including the *New York*

Times bestseller *Networking Is a Contact Sport: How Staying Connected and Serving Others Will Help You Grow Your Business, Expand Your Influence — or Even Land Your Next Job; Moving the Needle: Get Clear, Get Free, and Get Going in Your Career, Business, and Life;* and *After Further Review: How Reflection and Action Will Turn Your Somedays Into Today.*

93

QUESTION YOUR THOUGHTS AND EMOTIONS - DR. STEVE TAUBMAN

The Habit: Question your thoughts and emotions

By Dr. Steve Taubman – International Keynote Speaker, Empowerment Expert

Why: All of us, especially those who have been rewarded and acknowledged throughout our lives for being smart, have learned to believe in our minds. We think that if something occurs to us, it must be true. But the reality is we're all carrying mental baggage we didn't ask for, from our childhood and from significant or traumatic events of our lives. As a result, our minds often generate thoughts and emotions that don't serve us, that may even hurt us. Learn to distinguish thoughts and emotions that create suffering, and take a moment to step outside your mind to realize that just because you're thinking a certain way doesn't mean it's accurate or it's the only way to see it. My mantra is, "Don't believe everything you think." By applying this type of critical thinking to yourself, you'll be better able to extricate yourself from self–induced misery.

ABOUT STEVE: Dr. Steve Taubman's early years were plagued by crippling anxiety, depression, and low self–esteem. Despite graduating valedictorian from one of the nation's top chiropractic colleges and running a thriving practice, Dr. Steve found that his outer success did little to calm his inner turmoil.

Thus began a thirty–year journey to understand the root of his suffering. His exploration of Western psychotherapy, Eastern teachings of mindfulness, hypnosis, and the science of neurology provided profound insight into the universal nature and cause of suffering; the subconscious mind... which ultimately led to the creation of his successful UnHypnosis system and bestselling book.

Blending his teachings with a long time passion for comedy and magic, Dr. Steve developed a series of insightful, fun presentations about mastering the subconscious mind which was quickly embraced by organizations for their ability to get people in action.

A profoundly spiritual individual, Steve especially loves helping people translate their spiritual principles into useful tools for their day–to–day lives.

94

THE ITERATIVE PROCESS -
CHRISTOPHER BOLLENBACH

The Habit: Engaging in an iterative process for all pursuits

By Christopher Bollenbach – CEO of Bottega Louie

Why: I believe in an iterative process to achieve the best results from life. What does that mean? It means regularly engaging in repetitive activity that produces incrementally better results over time through transparent and truthful analysis. Let's take golf for instance. Now this sport has been a great joy for me and a great frustration in my life too! But why the frustration? There is an old saying that goes, "Practice makes permanent." In my past, I often approached my practice time in golf through an irregular schedule. My practice sessions consisted of working my way through the bag by hitting 20 or so balls per club. I thought I was being systematic (forgetting my irregular schedule). The truth is I was just going through the motions, and I was making a series of random practice sessions permanent. My experience with golf began to change when I started with setting goals per session, mid–term goals, and long–term goals. Then, I began analyzing my progress. When my growth faltered over time, I would try something new. Then I would track my progress. This going back and forth on repeated operating cycles paired with honest, thorough analysis has a good opportunity to become convergent. In other words, we can get closer to the desired result as the number of iterations increases. I find this process can be applied to EVERY endeavor in life. Anything I do gets better with an iterative process – interior home design, professional pursuits, raising my daughter, marriage, friendship, faith, and yes even golf.

This process creates the fabric by which I can work well with others as we pursue our mutual goals. Doing this allows us to forge a platform of mutually agreed upon, flexible performance objectives. In other words, we all know where we are going and are continuously evaluating how we can get there by honestly looking at how well we have done to date.

As you make this habit a regular part of your daily process, it will become innate. That's when the real magic happens. Once you reach that level, more of your aspirations will take shape.

ABOUT CHRISTOPHER: Christopher Bollenbach is the CEO of Bottega Louie and has been an active owner and investor since its founding in 2007.

A graduate of the Robins School of Business at the University of Richmond, Christopher began his career in finance on Wall Street in 1990. Throughout his career, he spent 25 years in finance and banking at UBS, PaineWebber, Merrill Lynch, and Citi Smith Barney and was most recently a Senior Vice President at Merrill Lynch. He also served as an executive for Sunkist Growers Inc. from 2001 to 2005.

Christopher has also served in a variety of executive management and directorship positions in hospitality, real estate development, tech, and agriculture.

95

MAKE YOUR ACTIONS SPEAK LOUDER THAN YOUR WORDS - ANGELICA BRIDGES

The Habit: Make your actions speak louder than your words

By Angelica Bridges – "Lt. Taylor Walsh", on the International Television Series, "BAYWATCH", Singer, Entrepreneur and Philanthropist

W**hy:** I have always been a big "doer" in life. I never liked to tell people about my plans. Let's not talk about what I'm gonna do or who I am. Why not, just show em?! Let someone FEEL who and what you are doing instead of hearing you do it.

Someone can tell me anything & make a million promises, but at the end of the day, it is all about some-one's true deliverance and action that makes a powerful statement.

I remember this saying...

"They May Forget What You Said, But They Will Never Forget How You Made Them Feel"

— Maya Angelou

I have always felt that goes right along with what this sentiment means to me in my life. Letting my actions show and speak for me is more powerful than any word I could ever speak.

About Angelica: The expression "multifaceted" is just one of the many ways to describe Angelica Bridges. Bridges, who hails from a small town in the USA (East Lynn, Missouri; pop. 150 people) and credits her most notably down–to–earth personality from being raised on a farm in the Midwestern countryside.

Bridges began her leadership and philanthropic aspirations at the age of 16, when she was crowned; "Miss Missouri Teen". A few years later she made her bold move to Los Angeles, California to pursue her entertainment and educational dreams while she attended *UCLA* as a Communications major.

Bridges is perhaps best known for her role as "Lt. Taylor

Walsh", on the international television series, **BAYWATCH**". The show would go on to become, "The Most Watched Television Show in the World." Bridges who finds great pleasure in entrepreneurial venture, enjoys wearing many hats effortlessly as an: *actress, television host, producer, chef, philanthropist, humanitarian* and most importantly; the proud *mom* of two young daughters.

Bridges serves on the Board of Directors for, "*The Gecko Group* spearheading a project that will create the first "eco–friendly, smart city" in the world (aka "His Majesty's Vision"), within the kingdom of Eswatini, Africa.

Bridges is also launching her custom signature dessert line, "**Gorgeous Goodies**" in the UK.

Bridges stars in, *"April's Flower's"* for *Lifetime Television*. She was on *"Kicking and Screaming"* for FOX. She reignited her character, Lt. Taylor Walsh in the Baywatch reunion movie, *"Baywatch Hawaiian Wedding"* also for FOX. Besides Brigitte Neilson; Bridges has been the only other actress to play *"Red Sonja"* on screen. Bridges has had recurring roles on *"The Days of our Lives," "The Bold and The Beautiful", "Mortal Kombat"* and *"Son of the Beach"*. She has also guest–starred on over 20+ television series.

Bridges was discovered by John Casablancas and went on to sign with *"Elite"*. Some of her most notable campaigns include: *Maybelline, Diet Coke, BMW, Geico, Hanes, Doritos, Nivea, Bally's Total Fitness, Lexus, Fruit of the Loom, Pontiac, Tab Energy Drink, Pepsi, Toyota, Miller Lite, Whiskas and*

Mitsubishi. She can easily be remembered in the *"Brut Cologne"* campaign with "NFL Hall of Fame" football hero, Troy Aikman. She was one of the first few females to ever represent the *"UFC"in* an ad campaign titled, "Beauty and The Beast".

96

FOLLOW THE "CARDIAC" ACROSTIC - RICHARD J. SHEMIN, M.D.

The Habit: Follow the "Cardiac" acrostic

By Richard J. Shemin, M.D. – Chairman of Cardiac Surgery and The Executive Vice– Chairman of Surgery at the Ronald Regan UCLA Medical Center

Why: As an Academic Cardiac Surgeon, I received my undergraduate and medical school education in an accelerated 6 year BA/MD program at Boston University. Then over 10 additional years I received surgical training at elite institutions eg Harvard, NIH, NYU, Stanford and the Kennedy School of Government.

Over the years, I developed essential habits to accomplish my responsibilities and allow myself to serve simultaneously in the many roles that I hold.

To give these habits structure, I created an acrostic from the word "Cardiac." This acrostic states my principles, philosophy, and habits for high performance. It is as follows.

C: Clarity of mission

A: Focused Attention

R: Relentless pursuit of excellence

D: Minimize Distractions

I: Integrity and Innovation

A: Affability and Collegiality

C: Exceptional and Ethical Care without Exception

As the current Robert and Kelly Day Professor of Surgery at the UCLA David Geffen School of Medicine, Chairman of Cardiac Surgery and The Executive Vice–Chairman of Surgery at the Ronald Regan UCLA Medical Center, Co–Director of the Cardiovascular Center and Director of Cardiovascular Quality, the use of all these habits is essential to my success and the highest level of performance.

Following the "Cardiac" acrostic gave me a road map to keep these habits at the forefront of my thought process. I feel that the "Cardiac" acrostic can be used by anyone in any field that needs to tap into consistent excellence in their area of expertise.

ABOUT DR. SHEMIN: Richard J. Shemin, M.D. has over 35 years of an active surgical practice. He directs a research laboratory. Dr. Shemin is the Director of a Cardiac Surgery Resident Teaching / Training Program. He is the Director of the Hospital and Medical School at UCLA. He handles these administrative responsibilities in addition to holding important national leadership positions in professional societies. Dr. Shemin holds the following titles.

- Robert and Kelly Day Professor

- David Geffen UCLA School of Medicine

- Chief of Cardiac Surgery

- Executive Vice –Chairman of Surgery

- Co–Director of the Cardiovascular Center

- Director of Cardiovascular Quality

- Ronald Reagan UCLA Medical Center

97

JUST SAY IT OUT LOUD! - JEREMY LANDON HAYS

The Habit: Just say it out loud!

By Jeremy Landon Hays – Actor, Writer, Producer

Why: I am a person who stutters. I was a very quiet kid. I avoided speaking unless I absolutely had to. Reading aloud in class or talking on the phone were nightmare scenarios for me. Most of my thoughts and feelings went unsaid simply because I was too afraid to try to express them. Luckily, in high school, a caring drama teacher encouraged me to audition for the school's Shakespeare play. Through acting, I gained confidence to speak even though I was afraid. My speech improved, but more importantly, I was heard! Whether you stutter or not, sometimes expressing yourself is just plain scary. I was afraid of being made fun of, judged, or dismissed for my stuttered speech. The fear of what others may think is something that we all share regardless of who we are. So, just say it out loud! And encourage others to do the same. Smile and feel proud that you dared to speak!

 **ABOUT JEREMY:** Jeremy Landon Hays is an actor, singer, writer, and producer. His television appearances include a recurring role on "The Oath" (Sony Crackle), "FBI" (CBS), "Broad City" (Comedy Central), "The Blacklist" (NBC) "Turn: Washington Spies" (AMC) and the soon to be released Scott Rudin project "Compliance" starring Mary Louise Parker. Jeremy is also set to appear in a new independent film Sometime Other Than Now. Jeremy recently played the role of Raoul, Vicomte de Chagny in Andrew Lloyd Webber's The Phantom of the Opera on Broadway. He made his Broadway debut in the first revival of Les Misérables and went on to originate the role of Enjolras for the 25th Anniversary production at Paper Mill Play-house and the subsequent national tour. He recently performed with the Chicago Symphony Orchestra at the Ravinia Festival as a soloist in Play It Again, Marvin a musical review of the music of Marvin Hamlisch. He toured the U.S. as Rum Tum Tugger in Cats. Regionally he has starred in productions of Into The Woods, Hair, Camelot, Thoroughly Modern Millie, Oklahoma! and West Side Story. Jeremy is proud to have represented Les Misérables on "The 85th Annual Academy Awards"

hosted by Seth MacFarlane as well as NBC's "America's Got Talent."

Jeremy is producing a new Broadway play "Paulette" by novelist, Mary Adkins. The play is currently in development in New York City.

Jeremy has been tapped to pen the book for a new Broadway musical adaptation of the Thomas Hardy novel *Far From The Madding Crowd*.

Jeremy has written two screenplays which are in development. "Buried Deep" is a modern western drama series set in rural Oklahoma. "Take The Black" is a comedic, mockumentary web-series about a down-on-their-luck band of cater waiters who have been recruited by the CIA.

Jeremy also founded the non-profit, non-partisan organization Broadway Votes which promotes voter registration and political involvement in the Broadway community.

98

ENGAGE IN A VARIETY OF DISCIPLINES - DAVID SILVERMAN

The Habit: Engage in a variety of disciplines

By David Silverman – Animator for the Simpsons, Director of The Simpsons Movie, Co–Director of Monsters Inc.

Why: Enthusiasm and curiosity about any subject, process, art form, science, history – you name it – can only help expand your mind and creativity. The more you engage in a variety of disciplines, the more you will have to draw upon to develop your own ideas. The juxtaposition of different concepts is what makes for advancement in all fields, from science and technology to arts and entertainment. The information gained from what you learn and experience is the fuel of creativity. And you never know where inspiration may come from. The more you gather, the better your chances for that eureka event. So there's no time for boredom, it's just a great big fascinating world out there to wrap around your brain.

 **ABOUT DAVID:** David Silverman is an animator and director, best known for his work on The Simpsons. David has been involved with the series from the very beginning, animating on all of the original Simpsons shorts for The Tracey Ullman Show. He went on to serve as Supervening Director of Animation for several years and currently serves as a producer. He has directed numerous episodes, as well as directing The Simpsons Movie.

In 2012 David directed the theatrical short Maggie Simpson in The Longest Daycare, which was nominated for an Academy Award for Best Animated Short Film.

Other film work includes Monsters, Inc. (Pixar) for which Silverman was a co–director. He has also worked on the animated films The Road to El Dorado (DreamWorks), Ice Age and Robots (Blue Sky), and Looney Tunes: Back in Action (WB).

David plays the tuba and has performed his flaming sousaphone at events like Burning Man. He is currently a member of the LA band Vaud and the Villains, and the Sea Funk Brass Band.

99

EMBRACE CHANGE - LEA WOODFORD

The Habit: Embrace change

By Lea Woodford – Author, International Speaker, Entrepreneur

Why: Change is inevitable. Nothing in life ever stays the same. As a military brat we had to move every two and a half years, I was always the new kid in school. While I didn't like this growing up, it has helped me foster some pretty important skills. When you are forced to move all the time you learn how to make friends and establish relationships pretty easily. Embracing change has also allowed me to transition through some of life's most difficult challenges such as cancer, divorce and a layoff after a merger.

We have seen what has happened to iconic companies

such as Oldsmobile, Woolworths and Blockbuster when they don't change with the times. Change is inevitable but accepting it and embracing it allows for new opportunities and often an amazing adventure.

My company has continued to change and evolve as our culture and target demographic has. It meant new skill sets were required and further education was necessary. With new skill sets it meant new opportunities as well as new revenue streams.

ABOUT LEA: Lea Woodford is the CEO of the SmartFem Media Group, full-service digital marketing, and advertising company.

As a sought after, International Speaker, Lea draws from her leaves, sharing her inspirational stories with grace and humor while focusing on leadership, innovation, and change to drive business, as she engages audiences and fosters a 'Think Bigger' mentality. Taking you through the journey of developing her online magazine and creatively growing it into the digital marketing and advertising company it is today, Lea motivates her audiences, in the same manner, she motivates her team; with her "Find Your Voice" mantra. As she 'walks her talk,' Lea encourages people to be bolder in their businesses and demonstrates how successes, as well as so-called failures, are an integral part of growing with intent in the right direction while consistently bringing a fresh approach and perspective on marketing, leadership, innovation and customer service.

Lea's expertise in online marketing and social media allows her to assist companies with the latest trends and help move them to the next level in the ever–changing digital space, imparting valuable information in a fun and entertaining way which leaves audiences motivated and ready to take action!

100

ALWAYS STRIVE FOR ALIGNMENT - MAT SHAFFER

The Habit: Always strive for alignment

By Mat Shaffer – International Coach and Speaker

Why: Alignment: it isn't just for tires anymore! If you want to be joyously empowered and effective in your life, everything gets to line up. Your career gets to be in alignment with your zone of genius and your passion. Your words and actions get to be in alignment with your values, vision, and integrity. Your relationships get to be in alignment with your heart and soul. Trust me, you'll feel it when things are clicking (and when they aren't).

One more important point - don't get attached to what alignment looks like in any area of your life! Whether you recognize it or not, you are always growing and evolving, and as you transform...what is right for you changes too. So check in with yourself often, and be willing to shift or walk away from any aspect of your reality that no longer fits. Consistently strive for alignment, and you will have an authentic, connected and successful life that serves as an inspiring example of what's possible for the countless people who believe they need to conform or settle to "matter" and feel good about themselves.

 **ABOUT MAT:** Mat Shaffer is a transformational speaker and empowerment coach for women who has dedicated his life to inspiring others to step into the infinite possibilities waiting on the other side of their fears and false beliefs.

Mat draws upon his undeniable passion and remarkable journey to shift audiences and clients across the world. He spent over a decade as a successful trial attorney and restaurant owner before experiencing profound spiritual and emotional awakenings, which connected him with his deepest purpose as an ardent advocate for authentic, empowered conscious living and deeper connected relationships.

Mat serves the world speaking from stage and online sharing his emotional intelligence insights and the lessons learned along the leadership path. He helps thousands of clients and students take their personal and professional lives to the next level as a private coach and course facilitator, in addition to serving as a Senior Trainer for Ascension Leadership Academy in San Diego, California.

ACKNOWLEDGMENTS

We greatly appreciate the following contributors for offering their own 1 Habit™s to this book.

- Steven Samblis – Creator of 1 Habit, Celebrity Interviewer, Entrepreneur

- Dr. Greg Reid – Entrepreneur, Keynote Speaker, and Bestselling Author

- Dr. Tony Alessandra – NSA Speakers Hall of Fame member and Bestselling Author

- Frank Shankwitz – Founder of the Make–A–Wish Foundation

- Dr. Rebecca Heiss – CEO/Founder Icueity Professional Speaker, Author, Director Envision Media Partners

- Lt. Randy Sutton (Ret) – Founder/CEO of The Wounded Blue

- Marie Roberts De La Parra – Chief Emotional Officer

- Mark Tufo – International Bestselling Author

- John Davis – The Corporate Action Hero

- Eileen McDargh – Award–Winning Author and Speaker

- Dr. Todd Dewett – Author, Educator, Speaker

- Erik Therwanger – Founder of Think GREAT

- Billy Arcement – The Candid Cajun, Leadership Speaker and Consultant

- Mark Sanborn – International Bestselling Author

- Dr. Kathy Gruver – Author, Speaker, and Educator

- Joy Rains – Mindfulness Speaker and Author

- Linda Zander – Founder of Success Pros Online and the We Give Program

- Susan Sharp – Artist, Speaker, and Author

- John Ayo – Wellness Speaker and Author

- Rick Broniec – Facilitator, Coach, Speaker, and Amazon Bestselling Author

- Gaurav Bhalla – Ph.D. Transforming Businesses and Lives: Speaker, Author, Coach

- Bonnie Low–Kramen – Author of Be the Ultimate Assistant

- Robert Siciliano – Bestselling Author

- Joe Schmit – Speaker, Author, Award Winning Broadcaster

- Kelly Byrnes – CEO and President of Voyage Consulting Group

- Mike Wittenstein – IBM eVisionary and founder of StoryMiners®

- Jim Cathcart – Golden Gavel Award Winner, Cavett Award Winner, Author, NSA Hall of Fame Professional Speaker, Top 1% TEDx

- Mandy Bass – Success Coach

- Gary Gopar - Professor & Department Chair of Music, Internationally Acclaimed Trumpet Player

- Dr. Sue Morter – Founder of Morter Institute and Master of Bio Energetics

- Michael Gregory – International speaker, qualified mediator, and negotiator

- Ray Waite – Futurist, Speaker, Trainer, and Founder of Lighthouse Force

- Dr. Dain Heer - Energy Transformation Virtuoso, Author, International Speaker

- John Floyd – Speaker, Comedian, and Author

- Dianna Booher – Bestselling Author

- Alan Berg – CSP, Global Speaking Fellow

- Theresa Puskar – Founder of Edu–Tainment Productions

- Art Sobczak – Author, Speaker, Sales Trainer

- Brent Scarpo – Speaker, Life Coach, Producer, Writer, and Director

- Bill Jelen – Founder of MrExcel Publishing

- Mohamed Tohami – Bestselling Author and Entrepreneur

- Dr. Hassan Tetteh – Heart and Lung Transplant Surgeon

- Bridgett McGowen– Awarded International Professional Speaker and Founder of BMcTALKS

- Robert T. Whipple – Top 100 Leadership Speakers by Inc. Magazine

- Sean Glaze – Author

- Jeff Davidson – The Work–Life Balance Expert®

- Lea Woodford – SmartFem Media Group

- Diana Maux - Holistic Fitness Coach

- Merrick Rosenberg – Bestselling Author

- Mark Levit – Founder of the Citizen Professor Institute

- Robin Hoffman Haack – Founder and CEO of Clar8ty

- Kristin Smith: Life & Business Strategist, Author & Podcaster

- Jill Christensen – Employee Engagement Expert, Best–Selling Author, International Keynote Speaker

- Holly G. Green – Founder of The Human Factor, Inc.

- Chris Warner – Actor, Writer, Director, Producer, Voice-over Artist

- Motoe Haus – Techno Music Producer and International DJ, Author

- Steve Beckles–Ebusua – International Speaker, Trainer, Presenter, and Amazon Top 10 Best Seller

- Raymond Harlall - Founder of The Power of Collaboration Movement

- Rick Broniec– Owner, Transformational Adventures

- Lisa Braithwaite – Speaking Coach and Author

- Marc Griffiths – Motivational Speaker and Author

- Jason Hewlett – CSP, CPAE, Speaker Hall of Fame, Author and Leadership Expert

- Gail Rubin – Certified Thanatologist

- Darlene T. Carver – Educational Entrepreneur

- Brandon B. Kelly Ph.D., CPM –Founder of CEO Super Summit; Founder of National Association of CEO's, International Speaker & Author

- Mike Tankel – Partner/Optimist, To Be Continued

- Ted Ma– Keynote Speaker and Leadership Expert

- Abby Donnelly – Founder and CEO of The Leadership & Legacy Group

- Amy Leslie – CEO of Perspective Consulting

- Jonah White – Entrepreneur, Author and Public Speaker

- Naomi Bareket – Author, Speaker, & Success Coach

- Alvin Law – Motivational Speaker & Bestselling Author

- Daniel Levine – Trends Experts

- Katie Mares – Brand Experience Expert

- Dave Swanson – Keynote Speaker and Leadership Trainer

- Roy Smoothe – #1 Amazon / iTunes Author, Publisher, Speaker, and Branding Consultant

- Michelle Lee Skaletski–Boyd – Intuitive Medium & Best–Selling Author

- Tracy Litt – Certified Mindset Coach, RTT, and Author

- Greg Vetter– Author and Corporate Trainer

- Buck Jones – Corporate Trainer and Educator

- Van C. Deeb – Author, Entrepreneur, Motivational and Inspirational Speaker

- Craig Titley – EP/Writer Marvel's Agents of S.H.I.E.L.D, screenwriter Scooby-Doo, Cheaper by the Dozen, Percy Jackson

- David Meltzer – Keynote Speaker, Author, Business Coach and Entrepreneur

- Shawn Edwards – Co–Founder – African American Film Critics Association

- Tom Cronin – Producer and Co–Writer of The Portal Film and Book

- Erik Swanson – Author, Speaker, Habits & Attitude Success Coach

- James Whittaker – Author / Co–Executive Producer of Think and Grow Rich: The Legacy

- Sharon Lechter – New York Times Bestselling Author, Speaker, Mentor

- Jennifer and Stephanie Sutto – CEOs of The Glitter Twins

- Cort Davies – Future Cancer Survivor, Speaker, Producer, and Writer

- Jessica Radetsky – Founder of Broadway Hearts

- Joe Sweeney – New York Times Bestselling Author

- Dr. Steve Taubman – International Keynote Speaker, Empowerment Expert

- Christopher Bollenbach – CEO of Bottega Louie

- John Shin – Author, Speaker, Philanthropist

- Angelica Bridges – "Lt. Taylor Walsh", on the

International Television Series, "BAYWATCH", Singer, Entrepreneur and Philanthropist

• Richard J. Shemin, M.D. – Chairman of Cardiac Surgery and The Executive Vice– Chairman of Surgery at the Ronald Regan UCLA Medical Center

• Jeremy Landon Hays – Actor, Writer, Producer

• David Silverman – Animator for the Simpsons, Director of The Simpsons Movie, Co–Director of Monsters Inc.

• Mat Shaffer – Mat Shaffer – International Coach and Speaker

ABOUT THE CREATOR OF 1 HABIT™

 Steven Samblis created and compiled 1 Habit™ by bringing together 100 incredible Happy Achievers™.

Steve is the founder and CEO of Envision Media Partners and Envision Media Press. Steve began his business life as a stockbroker, ranking among the top 50 rookie brokers at one of America's largest firms. He has worked with Congress defending shareholder's rights. In 1990, Steve founded "The Reason For My Success," a company that sold self–improvement programs. As the company grew, it expanded into the production of audio and video programs.

Over the years, Steve has traveled North America as the keynote speaker and launched two public companies.

His companies, Envision Media Partners and Envision

Media Press, were founded with the mission "To Empower and inspire people to become Happy Achievers." The company produces, acquires, and distributes personal development, medical training, legal training, and corporate training content across multiple platforms with an emphasis on Immersive Virtual Reality as a learning platform.

Made in the USA
Middletown, DE
16 September 2019